A DICTIONARY OF HOUSING

A Dictionary of Housing

Jack Rostron and Michael A. Nutt

arena

Published by
Arena
Ashgate Publishing Limited
Gower House
Croft Road
Aldershot
Hants GU11 3HR
England

Ashgate Publishing Company
Old Post Road
Brookfield
Vermont 05036
USA

British Library Cataloguing in Publication Data

Rostron, Jack
    Dictionary of housing
    1. Housing – Dictionaries
    I. Title   II. Nutt, Mike
    363.5'03

    ISBN 1 85742 370 4

Typeset in Palatino by Raven Typesetters, Chester.
Printed and bound in Great Britain by
Biddles Ltd, Guildford and King's Lynn.

Contents

Foreword

The provision of housing in whatever form is essential to the well-being of all people. Its nature and administration has become a complex phenomenon, often described in terms which are difficult to understand.

In this dictionary we have attempted to describe and define the administrative, financial, legal and technical terms used in housing in a clear and concise manner.

We hope that this book will be of value to professionals and students. As a reference book, used to increase understanding, it will be of benefit to housing providers and consumers alike.

Jack Rostron
Michael A. Nutt

Acknowledgements

The preparation of this dictionary would not have been possible without the assistance of several people. We are grateful to Mrs Norma Donakey, Mrs Phyllis Nutt and Miss Jennifer Rostron for typing the initial manuscript and reviewing numerous drafts.

We are especially grateful to Miss Anya Ahmed BA MSc MCIH for making invaluable additions regarding the definitions concerning housing associations.

We would also like to thank Mrs Josephine Gooderham, the Arena editor, for reviewing various drafts and making very useful suggestions regarding the legal aspects of the dictionary.

Finally, the project would not have been possible without the continuing support of our colleagues in the School of the Built Environment, Liverpool John Moores University.

Jack Rostron
Michael A. Nutt

A

abatement
1. Cancellation or reduction of a debt, e.g. a lease, providing for the abatement of rent.
2. The termination of a public or private nuisance.

abatement notice
1. A notice served on the owner or occupier of property regarding a private nuisance informing the person of the intention to abate the nuisance.
2. A statutory notice served under the Public Health Act 1936 by the local authority requiring a person to cease the nuisance.

abatement of nuisance
An alternative to a legal action which an occupier of land may invoke, by his own act, any nuisance by which that land is injuriously affected, e.g. cutting off the branches of a tree. Notice is required if entry is necessary to adjoining land.

abatement of purchase-money
Reduction of purchase price when a vendor misdescribes property and is unable to convey it as so described.

abode
The place where a person usually lives and sleeps.

abortive expenditure
Investment which has not achieved its purpose or has otherwise been wasted.

absolute covenant
A positive or restrictive covenant, sometimes called a qualified covenant.

absolute interest
Full and complete ownership of property.

absolute title
Registered owner of land guaranteed by the state under the Land Registration Act 1925, which is the principal statute concerning the registration of an interest in land.

absorbent quilt
See insulation quilt.

absorption
The property of a material to allow water to enter into it (i.e. to be absorbed). *See also* porosity, permeability.

abstraction of water
The withdrawal of water from a natural water supply, e.g. an aquifer. The abstraction is normally granted by licence from the statutory water authority.

abut
To border on, or adjoin, another piece of land or property.

abutment
1. The point at which a building provides some means of lateral support to another.
2. A brick or stone support to an arch such as a wall or pier.

ACC
Association of County Councils – a representative and pressure group for rural authorities.

acceleration
A future interest in land coming into possession, e.g. the surrender of a lease by a tenant, thereby accelerating the landlord's reversion.

acceleration clause
Part of a mortgage deed which gives the right, in certain stated circumstances, to repay an outstanding debt earlier than stated in the mortgage deed.

accelerator
A substance added to cement and plaster mixes (i.e. admixture) to speed the setting and hardening process. Generally used during cold-weather working conditions. *See also* gypsum plasters, keratin.

access
Approach or means thereof, eg. where there is a right of access to a highway by the owner of adjoining land.

access eye
See roding eye.

accessible dwellings
Residential units specially designed for occupation by people with mobility impairment, and who may need to use a wheelchair on some occasions. *See also* mobility housing.

accommodation agency
A commercial organisation which provides details of housing accommodation available for rent and is controlled by the Accommodation Agencies Act 1953, as amended.

accommodation stair
A stairway to provide access to floors and landings within a building. *See also* stairs.

accommodation works
Construction carried out by a local authority to other property belonging to the same owner with a view to reducing loss or damage to the latter property resulting from the acquisition. Normally undertaken on the acquisition of property by an authority exercising powers of compulsory purchase.

accounting order
In the housing association context the legal format with which it has to comply for accounting purposes.

accrued interest
Unpaid interest derived from a loan or an investment.

accumulative rate
Investment rate interest which is assumed, or known, at which an annual sinking fund will grow.

ACE
Association of Consulting Engineers – the professional association representing the interests of chartered civil, mechanical and electrical engineers.

acoustics
Sound quality and requirements in a room. Special acoustic materials such as plasters, boards and tiles to control sound insulation are available. *See also* insulation quilt.

acquiring authority
A government department, or local authority, using its statutory power of compulsory purchase.

acrow prop
A hollow steel pole that can be adjusted in length and is used as a temporary support.

ACS
Arrears and credit statement.

action
A civil legal proceeding started by a writ of summons.

action area
An area designated by a local planning authority for comprehensive redevelopment, rehabilitation or development within a prescribed period.

act of god
An incident resulting from a natural cause so devastating that it is beyond reasonable anticipation, e.g. earthquake, flood, landslide etc.

Act of Parliament
A statute containing laws which all persons must abide by. *See also* enabling Act or statute.

ADC
Association of District Councils

additive
See admixture.

adhesive
A material used to bond together the surfaces of two materials. *See also* mechanical adhesive, specific adhesive.

admixture
A plasticiser added to a concrete or mortar mix to produce workability and reduce voids (air space) in the finished product.

ADP
Approved Development Programme – a term used by housing associations.

adverse possession
Occupation of land without lawful title. *See also* squatter's title.

advertisement
Certain types of advertisements require permission under the Town and Country Planning Act 1990, as amended. The Secretary of State is empowered under this statute to make regulations controlling the display of advertisements, as far as it appears to be expedient in the interests of amenity or public safety. A wide range of advertisements is exempt from the need for formal consent, but permission is required for agents' boards above a certain size.

aerated concrete
A method used for producing lightweight concrete blocks

which have good thermal insulation properties. A controlled quantity of additive, such as aluminium powder, is included in the mix; this produces gas bubbles creating a finished product with a cellular structure.

affordability ratio
Rent to income ratio.

affordable rent
A term used in the housing association context relating to assured tenancies as a means of keeping rent levels within the means of low income tenants.

Age Concern
A charity established to look after the needs of the elderly.

agency board
A board displayed outside premises advertising it for sale or to rent, usually containing the name of the estate agent. There are restrictions on the size and number of boards which can be displayed. The maximum permitted area for a board displayed on a residential property is 0.5 square metres for a single board and 0.6 square metres for two boards joined at an angle.

aggregate
A material which is used in the production of mortars and concrete. *See also* fine aggregate, coarse aggregate, lightweight aggregate.

Agrément Board
An independent body, based at the Building Research Establishment, which tests and assesses new building products at the request of manufacturers. They issue certificates (Agrément Certificates) to indicate that a particular product complies with their specified requirements. *See also* performance specification.

Agrément Certificate
See Agrément Board.

agricultural drain
See land drain.

AGM
Annual general meeting.

airborne sound
Sound which is transmitted through air. *See also* structure-borne sound, sound insulation.

air brick
A special perforated brick built

into an external wall to allow air to enter a building for natural ventilation purposes. It is commonly used to provide air circulation to the underside of suspended timber ground floors. *See also* brick, hollow ground floor.

air conditioning

A system used to control and change humidity within a building to give an acceptable and comfortable living indoor environment. *See also* dehumidifier.

air entrained concrete

Concrete produced by a method which gives a consistent dispersion of bubbles throughout the mix, thereby improving workability and frost resistance to the hardened concrete. *See also* concrete.

air test

A test on a foul and surface water drain generally carried out on drainage runs between inspection chambers and consisting of blocking one end of the drainage run and pumping air in at the other end. A pressure reading is then taken from a special 'U' tube which should not fall below a certain figure if the drain is watertight. *See also* hydraulic test, smoke test.

alabaster

A gypsum-based mineral which is white and semi-translucent in form. Used for internal decorative finishes, e.g. on walls and columns, as a substitute for a marble finish.

allocation to a housing association

The amount of money provided by the Housing Corporation for capital expenditure to be expended in the forthcoming year.

allowances

The estimated amounts a housing association will spend on maintenance and management. The estimate is used in the calculation of the housing association grant provided by the Housing Corporation.

alloy

A metal modified by adding another material, e.g. adding carbon to iron to produce steel which has stronger properties than iron.

alternative dispute resolution (ADR)

A phrase which describes various types of mediation and conciliation of a dispute without recourse to litigation.

aluminium
A pure metal element used to produce aluminium alloys which have good durability properties and are highly resistant to corrosion. These are used to manufacture such items as doors and windows.

aluminium foil
A thin layer of aluminium which is used as a vapour barrier and radiant heat insulator. *See also* foil-backed plasterboard.

AMA
Association of Metropolitan Authorities.

amortisation
The writing-off of the capital cost of a wasting physical asset by means of a sinking fund.

amortisation rate
The rate of interest used for calculating amortisation.

amortisation term
The number of years applied to the useful life of an asset over which its value is written off.

ancient lights
Right of access to light to a building enjoyed for 20 years without interruption, when the right becomes absolute.

Ancient Monuments and Archaeological Areas Act 1979
This Act requires the Secretary of State to prepare a schedule of monuments which appear to him/her to be of 'national importance'. (This could include almost any building structure or site of archaeological interest made or occupied by man at any time.) The Secretary of State would be advised by English Heritage and the Ancient Monuments Boards for Scotland and Wales. The fact that a monument is scheduled does not mean that it will be preserved at any cost. It does ensure, however, that full consideration is given to the case for preservation if any proposal is made that will affect it.

ancillary use
A term used in town planning which describes the use of a property in a manner that is different from its main use.

angle bead
A metal, timber or plastic strip

placed at an external angle between plaster surfaces to reinforce the edge.

angle iron
A length of mild steel with an L-shaped cross-section. May be used as a supporting member, e.g. supporting a brick soldier arch above a door or window opening.

angle of repose
The maximum angle at which a heap of excavated soil will remain stable.

anhydrous gypsum plaster
A Class C gypsum plaster, used for general interior plasterwork, which is slow-setting and requires the addition of an accelerator to speed up setting time. *See also* gypsum plasters.

annual percentage rate (APR)
A term used to denote a stated rate of interest which takes account of the amounts and dates of repayment of capital and other disbursements associated with the loan. The Consumer Credit Act 1974, as amended, requires the publication of APR to prospective or existing borrowers.

annual value
The value placed on land for rating purposes. The gross value is the rack rent, i.e. the rent per year on the open market, less the landlord's costs incurred in paying for insurance, repairs etc. The net annual value, or rateable value, is the gross value less statutory deductions. Under section 837(1) of the Tax's Act 1989 it is defined as follows: 'Shall be taken to be the rent which might reasonably be expected to be obtained on a letting from year to year if the tenant undertook to pay all usual tenant's rates and taxes, and if the landlord undertook to bear the cost of the repairs and insurance and other expenses, if any, necessary for maintaining the subject of the valuation in a state to command that rent.'

annuity
An amount of money paid annually to a recipient during their lifetime. It is usually paid via a pension scheme.

anodising
A process used to produce a decorative or protective coat on a metal surface, (e.g. anodised aluminium).

anti-siphon pipe

An open pipe connected to a waste, soil, or soil and vent pipe and to which waste and soil appliances are connected. Its purpose is to prevent the water seals to such appliances being drawn out by siphonage. *See also* siphonage.

apex

The point at which two roof slopes meet at the top. *See also* ridge board.

appeal

A referral to a superior authority or court, or a judicial or administrative review of the decision, by an inferior body. An example would be an appeal to the Secretary of State against refusal of planning permission.

appendant

A subordinate interest or right attaching to a larger interest in land which, by virtue of law, will automatically pass with the conveyance of the greater interest.

appointed day

The day on which an Act of Parliament comes into operation.

appraiser

A person who determines the value of property. Normally called a valuer in the United Kingdom.

Approved Development Programme (ADP)

The Housing Corporation's cash limit for capital expenditure on different types of project for each financial year, approved by the Secretary of State for the Environment. After this the Housing Corporation allocates its funds to individual regions and housing associations. ADPs are also granted by the Secretary of State to some local authorities which fund programmes of housing association activity.

approved inspector

Under the Building Regulations a person who is approved by the Secretary of State or a designating body to supervise building work under powers conferred by the Housing and Building Control Act 1984, as amended. The statute establishes standards concerning the construction of buildings. All building work has to meet these standards and be approved by the local authority or an approved inspector.

arbitration
The determination of a dispute by a third party. A procedure favoured in property disputes avoiding the need for the normal litigation process. Arbitrations are of three types: statutory, commercial and county court. The decision of the arbitrator is binding except in exceptional circumstances.

arch
A method used to support the load and walling above the head of an opening. Arches may be curved, semi-circular, elliptical, segmental or flat (soldier arch, flat gauged arch), to reflect the design of the building. Arches are constructed of brick or stone consisting of individual units shaped to support each other and to transfer the load to the points of support (i.e. abutments). *See also* soldier arch.

architect
A person who designs buildings and is qualified by virtue of the Architect's Registration Act of 1934, as amended. It is an offence under the Act for someone to call him or herself an architect unless their name appears on the register maintained by the Architects Registration Council of the United Kingdom, which is the regulatory body established under the Act. *See also* design team.

architect's certificate
The certificate issued at various stages of construction by an architect, normally in accordance with the release of funds to a contractor on completion of various stages of work. *See also* quantity surveyor.

architect's instruction
A written instruction specifying alterations or additions to the building contract. *See also* variation order.

architrave
A moulded strip of timber used to cover the joint between the edge of wall plaster and a door frame or lining.

arch stone
An individual wedged shaped brick or stone used to form an arch, and also called a voussoir.

ARCUK

Architects Registration Council of the United Kingdom. It is unlawful for a person to call themself an architect unless his or her name appears on the register.

area of archaeological importance

An area designated under the Ancient Monuments and Archaeological Areas Act 1979, as amended, being one of archaeological importance so designated by the Secretary of State or local authorities. It is an offence in such areas to carry out, or cause or allow to be carried out, operations which disturb the ground or involve flooding or tipping without serving an operations notice on the local authority or unless specific exemption is granted.

AR19

A proforma which housing associations registered as Industrial and Provident Societies are required to complete and return each year to the Registrar of Friendly Societies.

arrears

Unpaid sums of money – normally rent that has not been paid on the due date. The terms for payment are normally stated as set periods in the lease agreement.

arris

The external angle or edge to a building unit, such as a brick.

articles of association

The document stating the duties and rights of directors and members of a company in relation to its organisation and administration.

artificial light

Light produced by electromechanical means from a lamp or bulb.

artificial stone

A mixture of crushed stone and cement manufactured in slab or block form to resemble natural stone.

asbestos

A silica-based mineral fibre mixed with cement (asbestos cement) which was used to produce a variety of building components such as pipes and roofing sheets with high fire-resistant properties. Due to the now known health risks involved in the manufacture and construction of asbestos components, substitute products are now manufactured using fibres of plastic, glass and textiles.

asbestos cement
See asbestos.

ashlar (ashler)
A wall constructed of square cut stone which is laid and bonded in regular courses with thin mortar joints.

asking price
The price stated by the vendor of a property which is placed on the market for sale. The eventual price may be less than the asking price.

asphalt
A material used for waterproofing large areas such as basements. Natural asphalt is mineral based and impregnated with a bitumen (e.g. lake asphalt from the West Indies, rock asphalt from central Europe). Mastic asphalt is a synthetic material produced from a mixture of bitumens and fillers such as stone dust, sand and crushed granite. *See also* tanking.

assembly of land
The assembling of individual parcels of land to form a larger unit normally for the purpose of developing the greater unit created.

assessment
The determination of a person's liability for various taxes, normally undertaken by an Inspector of Taxes.

asset
In terms of capital gains tax, the form of property including options, debts and other forms of property created by the person disposing of it.

asset valuation
The determination by expert opinion of the financial worth of the property which is often incorporated into company accounts.

assignment
Transfer of an interest in property from one party to another. Often associated with a lease.

assignor
A person who makes an assignment.

association investment profile

The Housing Corporation summary record of a housing association's overall performance. It forms part of the investment file used by Housing Corporation staff to establish whether a particular housing association is eligible for further capital funding.

Association of Metropolitan Authorities

A pressure group for metropolitan authorities.

assured shorthold tenancy

A tenancy granted under the Housing Act 1988 for a minimum of six months. The landlord cannot determine the tenancy during the initial six months.

assured tenancy

A tenancy under the Housing Act 1980, as amended, where the tenant has security of tenure.

attendance allowance

An allowance under the Social Security Act 1975, as amended, payable to disabled people who require constant attendance.

attic wall

An internal wall that projects into the roof space and is used as an extra means of support to rafters and purlins.

attornment

The transfer of property following a sale.

auction

A system whereby an auctioneer offers property for sale, selling to the highest bidder. A contract is made when the hammer falls in response to a final highest bid.

auctioneer

A person who conducts an auction.

auger

A mechanical or hand-operated device for drilling holes in timber, for extracting soil for sampling or for pile foundations.

automatic flushing cistern

A cistern that fills with water continuously and flushes automatically when the water level reaches a certain level. *See also* cistern, low-level flushing cistern, flushing cistern, water closet.

automatic level

A level which adjusts itself automatically. *See also* level.

award

An award normally made by an arbitrator after the consideration of the dispute between two parties, e.g. rent review.

axial load

A load which is centrally supported by a load-bearing structure such as a foundation. *See also* load.

axonometric projection

A drawing produced to give a three-dimensional view of a building and where all horizontal lines are drawn at an angle of 45°. *See also* isometric projection.

B

backactor
A machine used for excavating foundation trenches and bases. It can be fitted with various width buckets which scoop out the soil, either depositing it on the ground or loading it directly into a lorry.

back boiler
A metal box connected to hot and cold water pipes which is positioned in the back of an open fireplace and is used to heat water for washing and central heating purposes by means of solid fuel. Operates on a gravity feed principle rather than the mechanical means associated with other boilers. *See also* boiler, combination boiler.

back drop manhole
An inspection chamber used for connecting drains at different levels. *See also* inspection chamber.

backfill
Excavated material, such as soil, that is used to cover exposed groundworks, such as foundations, that have been completed.

back inlet gulley
A drainage gulley with an inlet incorporated at either the back or side into which a waste pipe is connected. *See also* gulley.

backland
A parcel of land which has no frontage to a highway.

back-to-back loan
A simultaneous transaction of property from one party to another secured by way of a loan.

bailiff
An officer entrusted with the execution of writs and processes issued from the courts.

balanced flue

A ventilating device, incorporated in a gas boiler, which is attached to an external wall to control the amount of fresh air entering and to allow exhaust gases to escape. *See also* flue.

balance sheet

A financial statement, of a particular organisation on a particular date, indicating the assets and liabilities.

balcony

An open area positioned at an upper floor level outside a building with access provided from inside by means of a door or window.

ball catch

A device used for closing cupboard doors and consisting of a spring-loaded metal ball which is fixed to the door and engages into a hole in the frame when the door is closed.

ball cock

See ball valve.

ball valve

A copper rod with a copper or plastic ball attached, which is connected to a water supply pipe to a WC cistern or water tank. The ball floats on the water inside and acts like a tap by switching off the water when it reaches a certain level.

baluster

A post fixed to the outer string and handrail of a stair and landing to form a balustrade.

balustrade

A row of balusters.

banker

One who receives money from customers to place on deposit and pays out following instructions from his customer. Usually an incorporated body which is regulated in the conduct of its business by the Banking Act 1987.

bankrupt

A person whose assets are invested in a trustee for bankruptcy following a declaration of bankruptcy in court.

bannister

A balustrade and handrail to a stair.

bargeboard

A timber board fixed to the

sloping edge of a roof and gable wall.

barrel bolt
A metal rod which slides into a keeper to secure a window or door.

barrel vault
A semi-circular arched roof or ceiling traditionally constructed of brick or stone, but now constructed of lightweight materials.

barrier free
Design principles which attempt to achieve a high degree of accessibility for physically disabled people.

basement
An area of a building situated below ground level and sometimes referred to as a cellar.

base rent
The lowest rent stated in, and payable under, a lease.

basin
See lavatory basin.

bath
A waste appliance in which a person's whole body is immersed for personal hygiene purposes. *See also* bathroom suite, slipper bath.

bathroom suite
A range of bathroom appliances including lavatory basin, wc, bidet and bath, all used for personal hygiene purposes. *See also* lavatory basin, bidet, bath, water closet.

batten
A thin strip of timber approximately 50mm × 25mm used to provide a means for fixing other components such as roof coverings.

battened door
Vertical timber boards fixed to horizontal timbers (ledged and battened door), and if necessary diagonal timbers (ledged, braced and battened door). Mainly used as an external door to sheds and outbuildings.

bay window
A window which projects beyond the external face of a wall. It may be curved, square or angle-shaped on plan. *See also* box window, bow window.

bead
A thin strip of timber which may

be rounded or moulded to cover a joint between two components such as a wall and window frame. Also used for glazing purposes. *See also* glazing bead.

beam

A structural member supported at each end and designed to support loads from walls, floors and roofs. *See also* main beam, secondary beam, simply supported beam.

beam and pile foundation

A foundation consisting of a reinforced concrete strip placed just below ground level (ground beam) supported by short plain concrete piles. Used to support the walls of buildings in subsoils liable to volume change, such as cohesive soils. *See also* foundation, raft foundation, strip foundation, ground beam.

bearing capacity

The foundation load a subsoil is able to support before it starts to compress.

bearing pile

A concrete pile that is supported on and transfers load directly on to a load-bearing strata. Usually pre-cast in one length or in sections and driven into the ground. *See also* displacement pile.

before and after valuation

The process under which property is valued in an existing state and thereafter when the property has been changed in some material way. Often used in association with town planning compensation, following a Revocation Order which is issued by the local planning authority rescinding a previously granted planning permission.

Belfast sink

A deep, rectangular glazed stoneware kitchen sink. *See also* sink.

benching

The concrete base to an inspection chamber, which is shaped and rounded into the channel.

benchmark

A fixed point from which the levels of a building are determined during construction. It may be an Ordnance or temporary benchmark. *See also* Ordnance benchmark, temporary benchmark.

bend
A term generally used to describe a curved pipe used for drainage, water supply and waste disposal.

bib tap
A tap connected directly to a water pipe and positioned above an appliance, such as a sink.

bill of quantities
A document prepared by a qualified quantity surveyor in accordance with the current Standard Method of Measurement for Building Works and used by the contractor for tendering purposes. It contains an itemised format of the labour, plant and materials required to construct a building and forms part of the contract documents. *See also* design information, quantity surveyor, contract documents, standard method of measurement.

bill of sale
An instrument used for transferring title.

bitumastic felt
A combination of woven fibres impregnated with bitumen obtainable in rolls for use as a damp-proof course or in sheets for use as a waterproof covering to flat roofs, or as an underlay to pitched roof coverings. *See also* built-up felt roofing, sarking felt.

bitumastic paint
Paint containing bitumen and used for waterproofing surfaces.

bitumen
See asphalt.

Black and Minority Ethnic Housing Association Strategy
A strategy devised by the Housing Corporation in 1986 which aims to promote black and minority ethnic housing associations.

blinding
Either a layer of thin concrete placed on soil to give a clean level surface to fix reinforcement, or a fine clean material, such as sand, used to fill in voids in the top surface of hardcore to provide a smooth surface to prevent damage to a damp-proof membrane.

block
A building unit normally manufactured from concrete, glass or

hardwood for use in the construction of walls and floor finishes.

block A properties
Housing developments built before the introduction of the Housing Act 1988 Housing Association Grant, which are not eligible for major repair housing association grant funding and have to rely on sinking funds set up from rent surplus fund transfers.

block B properties
Housing schemes developed prior to the Housing Act 1988 which are still eligible for major repair housing association grant funding.

blockboard
A composite timber board consisting of strips of timber sandwiched between two sheets of thin plywood, the whole glued together to form a standard-sized sheet in various thicknesses. Mainly used for general internal joinery work. *See also* laminboard.

block floor
A solid concrete floor covered with hardwood blocks of oak or mahogany and arranged in a pattern.

block plan
A simple plan showing the delineation of buildings, and other physical features, on a particular site. *See also* location plan.

block width
The dimensions across a building measured wall-to-wall.

blockwork
Blocks arranged and bonded together to produce a wall. *See also* block.

board
A timber (softwood or hardwood) strip between 100mm and 150mm wide and 20mm to 25mm thick used as a floor covering, or a composite sheet such as chipboard, blockboard, plasterboard etc.

boarded door
See battened door.

boarded floor
A timber joisted floor covered with softwood boards which have tongued and grooved edges. *See also* tongue and grooved boards.

boarding house
A private dwelling used for the purposes of short-term accommodation, which also provides meals, cleaning, etc.

body of deed
The part of a deed offering explanation but excluding recitals.

boiler
An appliance used for heating water for washing and central heating. Oil or gas is mainly used for firing the boiler and a pump would be incorporated on a central heating system to circulate the water. *See also* combination boiler, back boiler.

bolt
1. A metal device used for fixing components, comprising a cylindrical shaft with a fixed head at one end and a thread at the other to which is attached a threaded nut for adjusting and tightening the components being fixed.
2. Also a metal sliding rod or strap used to fasten and secure a window or door.

bona fide
A genuine act in good faith.

bond
Adhesion of two surfaces due to the application of an adhesive. *See also* adhesive.

boot lintel
A concrete lintel used to support a cavity wall above a door or window opening. It has a cross-section shaped like a boot so that the inner leaf is supported on the heel and the outer leaf on the toe with the cavity maintained.

bored pile
A concrete pile that is formed in situ by initially excavating out the soil, placing reinforcement and pouring concrete. *See also* friction pile.

borehole
A hole formed in the ground by extracting a core of soil for testing purposes.

borrowed light
A glazed area at the top of an internal doorframe or partition to allow passage of light from one area to another within a building. *See also* fanlight.

bottom rail
The bottom member of a panelled door.

boundary
The delineation, by way of a line, showing the separation of property in two separate ownerships.

bow window
A curved bay window. *See also* bay window.

boxed eaves
See eaves.

box frame
See sash window.

box gutter
A gutter having a rectangular cross-section and open at the top, which is usually incorporated at the edge of flat roofs adjacent to a parapet wall. It is laid to a gradient to dispose of surface water which drains into an outlet provided at one end of the gutter and connected to a rainwater pipe. *See also* gutter, eaves gutter.

box sash window
See sash window.

box window
A square-shaped bay window.

branch drain
A subsidiary drain which is connected to a main drain.

branch pipe
See junction pipe.

breach of contract
The non-fulfilment of the terms of a contract. The remedy is normally damages, specific performance, or rescission.

breach of trust
Where a trustee fails to carry out a duty.

breach of warranty
Where someone fails to comply with a contractual agreement.

break clause
The clause in a lease which gives the tenants and/or the landlord the right, in certain circumstances, to terminate the lease before its normal termination date.

break point
The date on which a lease terminates when a break clause is enforced.

breather paper
A waterproof paper used in timber-framed cladding in addition to a waterproof membrane. It also allows water vapour to escape, preventing condensation.

breeze blocks
See clinker blocks.

brick
A building unit used to construct walls. Manufactured from clay (clay bricks) or sand and lime (sand–lime or calcium silicate bricks). Clay bricks are classified as commons, facings or engineering bricks depending upon the quality required. Sizes of bricks were originally $9 \times 4\frac{1}{2} \times 3$" imperial; later, metric module bricks were produced (e.g. $290 \times 90 \times 90$ to fit a $300 \times 100 \times 100$ module). The usual size produced is now $215 \times 102.5 \times 65$. Brick is considered to be the most versatile building unit since it offers flexibility in the design of building components in terms of size, shape, colour and texture. *See also* air brick, clay bricks, common bricks, engineering bricks, facing bricks, pressed brick, wire cut brick, radial brick, refractory bricks, Roman brick, sand-faced brick, semi-engineering brick, sewer brick, silica brick.

brick bond
The arrangement of bricks to give a pattern and strength to a wall. The vertical joints between two bricks must be overlapped by the brick above. *See also* stretcher, half, English *and* Flemish bonds.

brick-on-edge coping
Bricks laid side by side on top of a wall so that the lengths of the bricks (stretcher faces) are on the top surface and the ends (header faces) are seen vertically from both sides. *See also* coping.

brickwork
Bricks arranged in a pattern and bonded together to produce a structure, such as a wall or pier. *See* brick.

bridging interest
1. Interest charged to cover a bridging loan between the sale and purchase of properties.
2. Interest chargeable on loans to cover expenditure by a housing association during the development of a housing scheme. The interest is normally funded from on-costs. *See also* capitalised interest.

bridleway
Highway over which the public has a right of passage on foot or horseback.

British Standards Institution

An organisation established by Royal Charter in 1929 with a view to regularising standards of the quality in materials, products and practices. Codes of practice established by the Institution ensure good standards of practice with regard to the manufacture and installation of materials, and design and workmanship. The majority of materials used for the construction of buildings are subject to British Standards with regard to testing and installation. *See also* Agrément Certificate.

brothel

A house used for the purposes of fornication by both sexes. It is an offence to keep a brothel.

browning plaster

See retarded hemi-hydrate gypsum plaster.

BSA

Building Societies Association.

buffer zone

A landscaped area separating developed areas. It is usually created to increase amenity and provide informal recreational space.

builder

A person or organisation responsible for constructing a building in accordance with the information provided by the architect. *See also* building contractor, contractor.

builder's quantity surveyor

See contractor's quantity surveyor.

building agreement

A contract between the owner of land and a developer, normally in the form of a licence whereby the developer agrees to construct buildings and on the due date is entitled to a lease of the land and buildings.

building by-laws

See by-laws.

building contract

A contractual agreement between the owner or occupier of land and a building contractor, indicating the terms and conditions under which the building is to be constructed.

building contractor

Someone who enters into a contractual agreement with an employer for the purpose of carrying out building or engineering works specified in the contract over the prescribed period.

building control
The process by which local authorities, or other approved agencies, approve and supervise the construction of works in accordance with the Building Regulations.

building depth
Maximum external dimension from the front to the rear walls of the building.

building frontage
See frontage.

building lease
1. A lease usually of 99 years' duration for a rent known as ground rent.
2. Where the lessee agrees to erect certain buildings which become the possession of the lessor on expiration of the lease.

building line
The delineation of a fixed distance from the centre of a highway in front of which building is not permitted. It is normally intended as a means to enhance the built environment and maintain road safety.

building paper
A heavy duty paper impregnated with bitumen to give waterproof properties and used as a lining in timber-framed constructions such as walls and roofs. It also may be used on top of blinded hardcore to prevent water absorption of wet concrete.

Building Regulations
A statutory instrument which lays down the approved methods of construction. They are administered by local authorities and other specified organisations. The Building Regulations 1991, as amended, cover the following matters: Structure; Fire Safety; Site Preparation; Toxic Substances; Sound; Ventilation; Hygiene; Drainage and Waste Disposal; Stairs, Access for the Disabled; Glazing; Heat and Energy.

Building Research Establishment
An organisation established to undertake research into methods of construction. The research undertaken varies from fundamental research to applied research in construction techniques.

Building Research Establishment Digests

Publications issued by the Building Research Establishment, usually on a monthly basis, which provide information on materials, techniques and applications used in construction. *See also* Building Research Establishment.

building services engineer

A specialist involved in the design and commissioning of services to a building such as heating, ventilation, electricity, water supply and drainage.

Building Societies Act 1986

This is the regulating legislation for building societies. This Act gave building societies new, wider powers directly to provide housing for rent and sale as well as extending societies' lending powers.

building society

An organisation established for the purposes of raising funds from its members to allow advances to be made to other members to purchase and build residential properties. They are non-profit organisations controlled by the Building Societies Commission and registered with the Registrar of Friendly Societies. Building societies are a major lender to housing associations.

buildings of special architectural or historic interest

Buildings which are listed of special architectural and/or historic interest under the Planning (Listed Buildings and Conservation Areas) Act 1990, which requires them to be subject to a special form of planning control intended to prevent the unrestricted demolition, alteration or extension without express consent from the local planning authority. *See also* listed building.

building survey

A report of the condition of an existing building carried out and prepared by a building surveyor.

building surveyor

1. Someone who undertakes surveys of buildings.
2. A qualified person who is mainly responsible for dealing with existing building stock in terms of maintenance, alterations, upgrading, conversion

and adaptation. *See also* surveyor.

built-up felt roofing
Bitumastic felt bonded in hot bitumen in three layers as a waterproof covering to flat roofs. *See also* bitumastic felt.

bulk density
The density of a material, such as concrete or soil, which includes any voids and water it may contain. *See also* density.

bulkhead
The ceiling above a stairwell.

bulking
The increase in volume of a material due to moisture or air.

bulldozer
A machine which has a large curved blade attached and is used for pushing loose material and for levelling and grading the ground.

bullnose step
The first step of a flight of stairs one end of which is rounded and fixed into a newel post.

bungalow
A single-storey residential dwelling.

business expansion scheme
An arrangement which allows individuals to secure tax relief after investing in a company involved in a particular type of business activity. Shares must be held for a minimum of five years to qualify for exemption from capital gains tax.

buttress
A projecting and attached portion of wall, running the full height, used for strengthening and design purposes. *See also* pier.

buyers' market
1. A situation in which the buyer has an advantage in purchasing property.
2. Where supply exceeds demand.

by-laws or bye-laws
Rules made by authorities for the administration, management and regulation of a particular area, undertaking etc., and binding on all persons coming within their scope.

By-laws are usually the means by which local authorities exercise some of their regulatory functions. They usually require the approval of the Secretary of State responsible.

C

calcium carbonate (C_aCO_3)

The main chemical compound of chalk and limestone used for the manufacture of lime plasters and cements. *See also* lime plasters.

calcium hydroxide ($C_a(OH)_2$)

Hydrated lime produced by slaking quicklime (calcium oxide).

calcium oxide (C_aO)

Commonly known as quicklime and is produced by heating limestone (calcium carbonate).

calcium silicate bricks

Bricks manufactured from approximately 90 per cent sand and 10 per cent hydrated lime, moulded into brick sizes and then steam heated in an autoclave, producing a smooth finished brick with sharp arrises.

Dyes may be added to the mix to produce a variety of colours. They are suitable for internal walls which are to be left exposed. *See also* brick.

calcium sulphate (C_aSO_4)

The main chemical compound of gypsum used for the manufacture of gypsum plasters. *See also* gypsum plasters.

calendar month

One of the periods of 28, 30 or 31 days in which a calendar year is divided. In leap years, a period of 29 days occurs in February.

calendar year

A period of 365 consecutive days, or in a leap year, 366 consecutive days including 29 February.

call loan

A repayable loan, redeemable in full on demand.

canopy
A projecting covering, such as a roof positioned to the outside of a door or entrance to a building.

cantilever
A projecting structure fixed at one end and capable of supporting a load.

capillarity
See capillary action.

capillary action
The movement of water between two objects that are close together, or through fine holes or pores of a material.

capillary groove
A space between two objects in the form of a groove to prevent capillary action. *See also* check throat.

capillary joint
A method of connecting two copper pipes by means of a copper sleeve containing a ring of solder at each end into which the pipes are fitted. Upon heating, the solder melts and then hardens to give a water-tight seal. *See also* compression joint.

capital appreciation
Increase in the value of a capital asset over a stated period, which is normally expressed as a percentage of the original value.

capital expenditure
Sums of money spent on improving and acquiring capital assets as distinct from revenue expenditure on such matters as maintenance.

capital gain
In terms of capital gains tax, the increase in value of capital assets as computed in accordance with the Capital Gains Tax Act 1979, as amended. Under the legislation, capital gains tax is payable when certain items are disposed of and at certain occasions. The most important occasions when tax may be liable are: first, when a person dies; second, when there is a transfer of chattels, property etc. between spouses when they separate; and, third, when an asset is donated to charity.

capital gains tax
A levy accruing to a taxpayer under the Capital Gains Tax Act 1979 and Finance Act 1984, as amended, following disposal of a capital asset.

capital improvement

Capital works undertaken on an asset with a view to enhancing its value. It does not include repairs or maintenance.

capitalised interest

Bridging interest accumulated on loans released during the development period. *See also* bridging interest.

capital money

Funds paid to trustees under the Settled Land Acts. Under the Act settled land is:

● limited in trust to any person by way of succession
● limited in trust for any person in possession
● limited in trust for a contingent estate
● limited to, or in trust for, a married woman
● charged with any rent charge for the life of any person.

The instrument by which land is settled is called the settlement.

capital receipts

In respect of local authority housing, money received from the sale of capital assets, mainly council housing and land. Currently central government controls how such funds may be used.

capital value

The capital value of an asset, as opposed to an annual or periodic value, such as rent.

capite, tenure in

Holding land directly from the Crown.

caravan

A mobile home which is capable of being moved from site to site. Normally used for short periods of time as a holiday residence.

Caravan Sites and Control of Development Act 1969

This Act gave local authorities new powers to control caravan sites, including a requirement that all caravan sites had to be licensed before they could start operating (thus partly closing loopholes in the planning and public health legislation). These controls over caravan sites operate in addition to the normal planning system, so both planning permission and a licence have to be obtained. Most of the Act dealt with control, but local authorities were given wide powers to provide caravan sites.

care and repair
A colloquial term describing agency services to assist elderly home-owners with housing maintenance, adaptations etc. *See also* staying put.

care in the community
A central government policy for releasing certain classes of inmate or patient from hospitals and institutions and arranging for care in the community.

carpenter
A craftsman who is responsible for fixing the structural timbers to a building such as roofs and floors. *See also* joiner.

carpentry
The work involved in fixing structural timber to a building. *See also* carpenter.

carriage
A timber member inserted under stairs and spanning from floor to landing to give support to treads and risers.

carriageway
A highway, along which there is a right to drive vehicles and possibly to lead or ride animals and to pass on foot, unless exempt by statute.

case
A court action, often referring to the particulars of a specific action.

casement fastener
A device for keeping a casement window closed.

casement stay
A metal strap attached to a casement window to keep it open.

casement window
A window incorporating a part that opens (opening light) for natural ventilation. *See also* top-hung window.

cash back
A sum of money paid by a property owner to a potential tenant in times of oversupply.

cash flow
Income and expenditure made during the life of a project.

cast in situ
A bulk wet material such as concrete placed directly in the required finished position on site. *See also* in situ.

category 1 housing
Defined in circular MHLG

82/69 as 'self contained dwellings to accommodate one or two older people of a more active kind'. This circular is no longer mandatory. *See also* sheltered housing.

category 2 housing
Defined in circular MHLG 82/69 as 'accommodation in grouped flatlets to meet the needs of less active older people'. The circular is no longer mandatory. *See also* sheltered housing.

Catnic
A tradename for a pressed steel lintel.

caulking
The process of filling a joint between two objects, such as drainpipes, to make it watertight.

caution
The Land Registration Act 1925 allows any person interested in land to lodge a caution with the Registrar, requiring notification of any dealings in the land. The Act introduced a system whereby all land in England and Wales is subject to compulsory registration on first conveyance

or sale of the freehold or grant of a lease for more than 21 years.

caveat actor
Let the doer beware.

caveat emptor
Let the buyer beware.

caveat subscriptor
Let the signer beware.

caveat venditor
Let the vendor beware.

cavity fill
Concrete placed in the cavity of a cavity wall up to ground level, the purpose of which is to direct water trapped in the cavity to the outside via drainage points provided in the outer leaf. *See also* cavity tray, weep holes.

cavity gutter
See cavity tray.

cavity sleeve
A lining used at the back of an air brick to bridge through a cavity wall to allow fresh air to enter. *See also* air brick.

cavity tie
A metal or PVC strip built into the outer and inner leaves of

cavity walls and shaped so that any trapped water falls clear and does not travel across. Metal ties must be non-cor-rodible.

cavity tray
A wide damp-proof course that is provided across a cavity wall and is sloped to direct water trapped in the cavity to the out-side via drainage points pro-vided in the outer leaf. *See also* weep holes.

cavity wall
An external enclosure to a build-ing comprising an outer leaf of bricks or stone, an inner leaf of concrete blocks, and an air space (cavity) with both leaves tied together with special ties. The external leaf would be in either facing brick or stone for appear-ance, and the inner leaf would be either an insulation block or a concrete block with the cavity filled with an insulation mater-ial and non-corrodible metal ties used to tie both leaves. *See also* wall, weep holes.

CECODHAS
European Liaison Committee for Cooperative and Social Housing. It represents national

member organisations in 16 European countries which are providers of social housing.

ceiling
The lining to the underside of an upper floor, as seen from the room below.

ceiling joists
Timber beams used to support a ceiling below and possibly required to support a floor above.

ceiling rose
An electrical junction fixed to a ceiling to which a light is attached or suspended.

ceiling value
The maximum compensation payable for compulsory acquisi-tions, normally associated with site value for unfit houses.

cement
A substance used for producing concrete and mortars. Acts as a binder or matrix in that it causes aggregates to adhere as a result of a chemical reaction when water is added. *See also* Portland cement.

cement grout
See grout.

cement mortar
See mortar.

cement rendering
See render.

cement screed
See screed.

centering
Temporary timber framework used to construct an arch.

central heating system
A method used for heating the whole building, in which water is heated by a boiler and circulated by pumping through pipes to individual radiators, or in which warm air is supplied by fans to rooms through ducts. *See also* space heating.

centre of gravity
The point at which a mass will balance.

centres
See centering.

ceramic tile
A clay tile which has one glazed surface giving high water resistance. Used for lining walls around baths and shower units.

certificate of making good defects
The certificate issued by an architect or surveyor under a building contract at the end of the defects liability period, indicating that the contractor has satisfactorily made good any defects. It has the effect of releasing the balance of retention money to the contractor.

certificate of practical completion
A certificate issued by an architect or surveyor indicating that works have been substantially completed and the building is ready for occupation. The certificate allows the release of an agreed percentage of retention monies.

certificate of value
A certificate signed and issued by the purchaser of property attesting the price paid, often for the purposes of stamp duty.

certificate, land
A document under the seal of the Land Registry which contains the particulars of a piece of land.

cesser
The premature cessation of a right or interest.

cessio bonorum
The surrender by a debtor of his property to his creditors.

cesspit
See cesspool.

cesspool
A tank placed in the ground into which sewage is discharged from buildings whose foul drains are not connected to public sewers. It requires emptying at regular intervals. *See also* septic tank.

chamfer
An external edge cut at an angle of approximately 45°.

change of use, material
See Use Classes Order.

channel
1. Half a drainpipe that is placed in the bottom of an inspection chamber.
2. A rolled mild steel U-section member.

charge
A form of security on land, by virtue of the Law of Property Act 1925, for payment of a debt, allowing the creditor to receive payment from the proceeds of sale. Under the Act the only property charges capable of subsisting are a rent charge or legal mortgage.

charge by way of legal mortgage
A legal charge introduced by the Law of Property Act 1925, as amended. It is a form of security for the payment of a debt or performance of an obligation. The property cannot be disposed of until the debt is paid.

charging order
A court decree imposing a charge on a debtor's property to secure payment of same, made under the Charging Orders Act 1979, as amended.

charitable housing associations
Housing associations are normally charities which are either constituted as charitable trusts or companies or industrial and provident societies.

charity
An organisation established for charitable purposes under the

Charities Act 1960, section 45(1), as amended. The Act requires all charities to be controlled by the Charity Commissioners.

Chartered Institute of Housing

The professional body for those engaged in the practice of housing management. Previously called the Institute of Housing Managers.

chartered surveyor

A professional surveyor who is a fellow or professional associate of the Royal Institution of Chartered Surveyors. The institution is divided into various divisions to which particular members belong.

chattels

Leasehold or other interest in land less than freehold interest. Sometimes called chattels real.

check throat

A groove incorporated in the underside of the projecting part of a window or door sill which allows water to fall clear. *See also* capillary groove.

Children Act 1989

The most recent legislative safe-guard for children. Its most relevant sections regarding housing are sections 20, 24 and 27 which require local authorities to ensure that young persons in need and under the age of 18 have access to accommodation and other services.

children's home

A home established under the Children Act 1989, as amended, which provides care for more than three children at any one time. It excludes circumstances where there is some parental responsibility.

chimney

A brick or stone structure which incorporates a flue, the purpose of which is to convey and discharge smoke from a solid fuel fire to the outside. *See also* flue.

chimney breast

The part of the wall that houses a fireplace and flue within a room. *See also* chimney.

chimney cowl

See cowl.

chimney pot

An ornamental circular clay or concrete pot placed on the top of a chimney.

chimney stack
See chimney.

chipboard
See particle board.

cill
See sill.

CIPFA
Chartered Institute of Public Finance and Accountancy.

circuit
A system of electric cables and equipment necessary for an electric current. *See also* current.

circulation ratio
The relationship between net internal area to gross internal area of a building expressed in terms of a ratio or percentage.

cistern
A tank used to store cold water for the purpose of supplying hot water and heating to a building. It is manufactured from galvanised steel and PVC and usually fixed in the roof space with water fed direct from a cold water feed pipe operated by a ball valve. *See also* flushing cistern.

civic trust
A voluntary organisation estab-lished in 1959 to promote the improvement and protection of the built environment.

civil
As opposed to criminal, military or ecclesiastical.

claim
The assertion of a right, such as when an event insured against happens.

claw back
The recovery, by lawful means, of the whole or part of the payment which is properly due at a time stated.

clay bricks
Bricks manufactured by either pressing clay in moulds or extruding and wire-cutting the clay to form the shape of the brick which is then fired and burnt in kilns to produce common, facing or engineering bricks. *See also* bricks, common bricks, engineering bricks, facing bricks.

clay roof tiles
Pitched roof covering, manufac-tured from burnt clays. Plain tiles have a slight camber to pre-vent capillary action and incor-

porate two nibs for hanging over roof battens and are fixed double lap. *See also* concrete roof tiles, Roman tile, pan tiles, lap, gauge.

clearance area

An area designated by a local authority for the clearance of buildings, where housing, especially, has been declared unfit for human habitation.

cleared site area

Under the Leasehold Reform Act 1967 as amended, a method of valuation using the direct comparison method. Comparison is made with other residential sites which have already been disposed of. The Leasehold Reform Act 1967 allows tenants on long leases the right to acquire the freehold.

clear height

The height between floor surface and lower parts of roof trusses, ceiling beams or haunches at the eaves.

clear span

The distance between the face of each support. *See also* span, effective span.

Clerk of Works

The architect's representative based on-site to ensure that the building is constructed in accordance with the contract documents.

client

Person or organisation requiring a building to be designed and constructed, and who appoints an architect to organise the project in accordance with his requirements. Some organisations, such as local and public authorities, employ their own architects.

clinker

The remains of burning coal in a furnace which may be used as a lightweight aggregate or for producing concrete blocks.

clinker blocks

Building blocks made from clinker and cement and may be used for building internal walls. Also known as breeze blocks.

clog on equity of redemption

A doctrine that no mortgage deed may contain a requirement fettering the mortgagor's right of redemption.

close couple roof

A couple roof incorporating a horizontal member connected to the bottom of the rafters to form a tie and capable of greater span. *See also* pitched roof, collar roof.

closed eaves

See eaves

closed stair

A stairway which is enclosed both sides by a wall. *See also* stairs.

closer

A brick that is cut to maintain the brick bond at openings and corners. *See also* king closer, queen closer.

close string

See outer string.

closing order

An order made under the Housing Act 1985, as amended, in respect of unfit dwelling houses which are beyond reasonable repair. The order prohibits the use of premises for any purpose other than that stated by the local authority.

coarse aggregate

Constituent part of a concrete mix which contributes to the strength and consists of either gravel or crushed rock. *See also* concrete.

code of measuring practice

A code developed for the measurement of buildings by the Royal Institution of Chartered Surveyors.

coefficient of thermal conductivity (K value)

A measure of the rate at which heat is conducted through a material and is used in calculating thermal resistance. It is expressed in W/m deg.(CS1 Unit). *See also* thermal resistance.

cohabitation

The practice of living together as husband and wife, even if not married.

cohesive soil

A soil containing a high proportion of clay which is subject to volume change (expansion and contraction) with the increase and drying out of water. *See also* subsoil.

CML

Council of Mortgage Lenders –

An organisation which represents the interests of mortgage lenders, such as building societies.

cold bridge
Part of a structure which has a different thermal insulation to the remainder, e.g. at the sides of door and window openings where a cavity wall has been closed causing a colder surface which may result in condensation occurring.

cold roof
A flat roof where the thermal insulation layer is placed within the ceiling resulting in cold air in the roof space which may cause condensation. *See also* warm roof.

cold water pipe
A pipe which carries cold water. *See also* cold water supply.

cold water storage tank
See cistern.

cold water supply
Pipes within the boundary and within a building which convey cold water from the mains or cistern. *See also* rising main.

collar roof
A close couple roof where the tie is fixed to the rafters approximately at one-third of the vertical height of the roof and allows part of the roof space to be utilised within a room. *See also* close-coupled roof, pitched roof.

collateral
The security given by the borrower to the principal or lender. *See also* secured loan.

collateral agreement
An agreement used by professionals employed by a developer, which places an additional duty of care to whoever purchases the development when completed.

column
A vertical structure used to support a beam from which the load is transferred.

combination boiler
A gas-fired boiler which heats cold water instantaneously and supplies hot water direct to appliances rather than from a hot water cylinder. It also heats water for central heating purposes and the system does not require a cold water storage

tank or hot water cylinder. *See also* multi-point water heater.

combined sewage system

Waste water from both foul and surface water drains conveyed in one sewer. *See also* Separate Sewage System.

commission

The fee of a professional adviser or agent for services provided, e.g. an estate agent who receives a fee for arranging the sale, or lease, of property.

Commission for Racial Equality

See race relations.

Commissions for Local Administration

Organisations established to investigate allegations of maladministration by local authorities.

committee of management of a housing association

The managing body of a housing association registered as an industrial and provident society and elected by its shareholders. It has ultimate responsibility for the affairs of the association and must have a minimum of seven members.

common assurances

Legal evidence to prove transfer of property, e.g. by deed, will etc.

common bricks

Cheapest and commonest variety of brick produced, banded in appearance in tones of yellow and pink having sharp arrises and a smooth texture. They generally have a hard outer shell but a softer interior which weathers rapidly once the outer shell is broken. They are therefore only suitable for internal use or walls in unexposed situations. *See also* brick, clay bricks, engineering bricks, facing bricks.

commonhold

A situation where the freehold of all common parts of a property is vested with all the owners and managed by a separate management committee. Commonly used by flat owners.

common law wife or husband

A man or woman who lives in a sexual relationship with a partner of the opposite sex in the same dwelling but is not married.

common rafter
A rafter that runs the full length of the roof from the ridge to the eaves. *See also* rafter, hip rafter, jack rafter, valley rafter.

common joist
A floor joist that spans the full floor length, i.e. clear span. *See also* joist, floor joist.

common parts
The parts of the building not let to individual tenants and normally retained by the landlord. Usually applied to parts of multi-occupied buildings.

common stair
See public stair.

communication pipe
A water pipe between, and connected to, the water authority's main at one end and the water pipe serving the building at the boundary.

community charge
A local tax now replaced by council tax.

community leasehold
A form of equity-sharing through housing associations. It is not the same as shared owner-ship in that occupiers do not have the right to acquire increasing shares in the equity of their homes. Rents are based on capital values and not fair rents.

community ownership
The process where a housing association or cooperative buys out a local authority estate.

community property
Property commonly owned between husband and wife.

compaction
The process of compressing a material to achieve density or strength. *See also* segregation.

company
A legal personality involving a group of individuals holding shares and who have a common purpose which is carrying out an activity through a business normally registered under the Companies Acts, which provides for three basic types of company:

● companies limited by shares, where the liability of members is limited by share value
● companies limited by guar-

42

antee, where the liability of members is limited to such amount as the members agree to contribute

● unlimited companies where there is no limit of liability.

A registered company is defined as a private company unless it registers as a public company with a share capital meeting the minimum requirements.

company registration
The requirement by the Registrar of Companies for certain types of company to register and receive a Certificate of Incorporation recognising its legal identity.

comparable
A particular property, land or transaction, providing evidence for the valuation of another property. The prior property having a similar nature to the one being valued.

compensation
Money paid under the Land Compensation Acts 1961 and 1973, as amended, to the owner and/or occupier of property in compensation for the curtailment or removal of their rights in a property, often awarded in association with compulsory purchase.

completion
Completion of a contract on the part of the vendor in conveying title and acceptance of same by the purchaser.

completion statement
A statement prepared by solicitors, normally for vendor and purchaser respectively, and made following the completion of the conveyance of a property.

component
Part of a building element which may be in situ or prefabricated.

composite board
A sheet made from a combination of materials such as foil-backed plasterboard and woodwool. *See also* foil-backed plasterboard, woodwool, particle board.

composition floor
A floor finish applied in a wet condition and spread on to a solid concrete floor to give a jointless construction. *See also* magnesite flooring, pitchmastic.

compound interest

Interest made at given intervals on accumulated interest and including the principal.

compulsory purchase

The compulsory purchase of land or property under an enabling statute for a stated public purpose. The process follows standard procedures contained in the Acquisition of Land Act 1981, as amended. *See also* notice to treat, Compulsory Purchase Order, vesting declaration.

Compulsory Purchase Order

An instrument facilitating the compulsory acquisition of land. Such instruments can only be issued for purposes specified in particular enabling Acts. *See also* vesting declaration.

compound settlement

A bundle of documents, often wills and deeds, extending over a period of time and constituting the means by which ownership of land is settled. *See also* settlement, strict settlement.

compression

Forces that act towards each other causing material to be squashed or shortened when a load is applied, e.g. the bending of a top portion of a beam. *See also* tension, shear.

compression joint

A method of connecting two copper pipes by means of a nut which is tightened causing a soft copper ring fitted to the ends of the pipe to compress to give a watertight seal. *See also* capillary joint.

compressive force

A force causing the fibres of a material to squash together. *See also* compression.

compressive stress

A measure of the force required to cause a material to be in a state of compression and is expressed in N/mm^2 and kN/mm^2. *See also* stress, compression, tensile stress.

concentrated load

See part load.

concrete

A mixture of fine aggregate (sand), coarse aggregate (gravel or crushed rock) and Portland cement in specified proportions to which water is added which reacts chemically with the cement to bind the whole mix together producing a hardened mass. *See also* aerated concrete, air entrained concrete, non-fines concrete, reinforced concrete, plain concrete, pre-cast concrete, pre-stressed concrete, in situ concrete, ready mixed concrete.

concrete blocks
Manufactured from aerated concrete and used for constructing the internal leaf of cavity walls and internal walls. *See also* aerated concrete.

concrete blinding
See blinding.

concrete roof tiles
Pitched roof covering manufactured from a fine concrete mix where the exposed face is sanded in a variety of colours. They incorporate nibs for hanging over roofing battens and are laid single lap so that their edges interlock with the adjacent tile. *See also* lap, gauge, clay rooftiles, Roman tile.

concrete strip foundation
See strip foundation.

concurrent interest
Two or more interests with joint ownership of land.

condensation
Moist air that forms water particles on a surface that has a lower temperature (dew point). *See also* surface condensation, interstitial condensation, dewpoint.

conditional contract
A contractual agreement which is subject to either a condition subsequent, or a condition precedent, or both.

conditional planning permission
A colloquial term describing the grant of planning permission with conditions attached.

conditions of sale
The conditions attaching to the sale of properties under offer. Two standards exist: first, the National Conditions of Sale; and, second, the Law Society's Conditions of Sale.

condominium
A development including two or more units, normally residential. The individual units, or parts thereof, are owned, but

other common parts are managed separately by an agreement of the owners.

conduction
The transfer of heat energy through a material from a point at high temperature to a point at low temperature. Metals conduct heat. *See also* convection, radiation.

conductivity
See coefficient of thermal conductivity.

conduit
A protective tube or cover into which electric cables are placed.

confirmation
The conveyance of an estate, whereby a voidable estate is made sure.

consent
Colloquial term used to describe when planning permission has been granted for development.

conservation area
An area designated under the Planning (Listed Buildings and Conservation Areas) Act 1990, as amended, by the local planning authority as being of special architectural and/or historic interest.

consideration
The sum payable by one party as part of a contractual agreement. Regarding property law, the term is normally applied to the price offered by the purchaser in a contract to acquire land or buildings.

consolidation of mortgages
The doctrine which allows a mortgagee with several mortgages by the same mortgagor on several properties to redeem all of them if the mortgagor seeks to redeem any of them. The doctrine is now repealed under the Law of Property Act 1925.

consumer credit licence
Under the Consumer Credit Act 1974, as amended, a housing association requires a licence if it wishes to offer credit brokerage services introducing tenants to sources of mortgage finance.

construction joint
A joint between two structures, such as two concrete areas, that have been placed in situ at different times.

construction period
The length of time taken from the start of construction to the completion of a particular building project. The completion date is often referred to as the date of practical completion and a certificate is issued by an architect to that effect.

contiguous
Common – as in a shared boundary.

contingency fee
An incentive fee which is paid in relation to the degree of success achieved in the task at hand.

contingency insurance
In an insurance contract, the protection offered on the occurrence of a risk, or other event, insured against.

contingent interest
An interest in land which comes into operation at some time in the future, often associated with a specific event.

continuous foundation
One which supports a load-bearing wall over its whole length.

contract
An agreement between two or more parties which is legally enforceable. For a legally enforceable contract to exist there must be:

- legal capacity of the parties to contract
- intention to contract
- valuable consideration
- legality of purpose and
- certainty of terms.

See also fixed price contract, prime cost contract, cost plus contract.

contract deposit
The amount paid by the purchaser of property under a contract and usually held by a solicitor. It indicates that the payer will fill his contractual obligations but, in the event of a default, he will forfeit the deposit.

contract documents
The documents which form the basis of a contract between the client and contractor and which include a formal signed contract by both parties and the design information (drawings, specifications and bill of quantities).

See also contract sum, contract period.

contract for sale of land
A written agreement signed by both parties. Where such agreements are exchanged one part must be signed by each party under section 2 of the Law of Property Act 1925, as amended.

contraction joint
A movement joint provided at a specific point in concrete or masonry constructions that allows for shrinkage to take place. *See also* expansion joint.

contract manager
A person employed by a contractor and who is responsible for managing the building work.

contractor
A building firm which is responsible for constructing a building in accordance with the contract documents. *See also* builder, building contractor.

contractor's quantity surveyor
A person who is responsible for dealing with all contractual and financial matters on behalf of the contractor, and prepares monthly and final accounts for agreement by the design team's quantity surveyor. *See also* quantity surveyor.

contract period
The time agreed by the contractor to complete the building in accordance with the contract documents commencing on a specified date (i.e. date of commencement) and completing on a specified date (i.e. date of completion).

contract sum
The sum of money agreed by the contractor to carry out the building works in accordance with the contract documents.

contractual improvement
The improvement of property carried out under a legally enforceable agreement.

contribution clause
The clause in an insurance policy which requires part payment of the losses suffered.

contributory mortgage
Where the mortgage advance is made to two or more parties. A trustee is precluded from receiving such an advance.

controlled tenancy

A dwelling house which has a protected or statutory tenancy where the rateable value did not exceed that stated in section 17(1)(a) of the Rent Act 1977. Controlled tenancies were converted to regulated tenancies under section 18A of the Rent Act 1977, as amended.

controlled ventilation

The provision of sufficient fresh air to a building area to prevent stagnant air and condensation forming, e.g. in roof voids. *See also* natural ventilation, mechanical ventilation.

convection

The transfer of heat energy through a liquid or gas by cooler heavier air causing warm air to rise. A system used in some electric fires and gas fires. *See also* conduction, radiation.

conveyance

The transfer of land under the Law of Property Act 1925, as amended.

conveyancer

A solicitor or barrister who specialises in conveyancing.

conveyancer, licensed

One authorised under the Administration of Justice Act 1985, as amended, to undertake conveyancing for profit.

conveyancing

The legal procedures involved in the transfer of title from one person to another.

Conveyancing Ombudsman

One who investigates complaints against authorised practitioners. Established under the Courts and Legal Services Act 1990, as amended.

co-op/cooperative housing

A housing association which is administered on cooperative lines so that its members/shareholders are the tenants or potential tenants. *See also* primary cooperative, secondary cooperative.

cooperative promotion allowance

Housing association grant allowance to pay certain costs when a primary cooperative receives services from another organisation, usually a secondary cooperative.

co-ownership

The situation where two or more people are entitled to the shared ownership of land, by either a joint tenancy or by tenancy in common.

coping

A capping used to shed water and protect the top of a wall. Materials used include brick and stone. *See also* brick-on-edge coping, saddle back coping.

copper

A pure metal element which is used for hot and cold water pipes and as an expensive roof covering.

corbel

A brick or stone projection from the face of a wall used as a means of support.

corbelling

Brick or stone projections which form a series of inverted steps used as a means of support.

core

The central part of a flush door which may comprise a lightweight material such as a box arrangement of cardboard or strips of timber to form a solid core. *See also* internal door, external door, fire door.

cornice

1. A moulding placed at the top of a wall to cover the joint between the wall and ceiling.
2. An ornamental projecting band of stone or brick on an external wall.

corporeal property

Land.

corrosion

The destruction of a material by the chemical effects of the atmosphere e.g. the rusting of metal.

cost floor

Under the right-to-buy scheme, the original cost of provision of the property. The discount allowable cannot fall below this cost floor.

cost of living clause

The clause in a lease or other form of property contract providing for the adjustment in rent price, or other financial item, based upon the retail price index.

cost plus contract

A building contract where the price is based upon the actual, or estimated cost, of the works, together with a proportion to represent profit for the contractor.

cost rent
A rental payment calculated to provide, over a period of time, a sum which is sufficient to meet the cost over the same time period of a notional loan interest, or actual interest.

council tax
Local property tax which replaced the community charge levied by local councils.

counterpart
A duplicate document of a legal nature often associated with the landlord's copy of a lease.

Countryside Act 1968
This Act replaced the National Parks Commission with a Countryside Commission which was given wider powers and improved finance. Local authority power was also expanded to include the provision of country parks and places intended for enjoyment.

couple roof
A roof comprising rafters to each roof slope with their ends fixed at the top (apex) and the bottom end supported on a wall (eaves). *See also* pitched roof.

covenant
An agreement contained in a deed and usually applied to an interest in land. It may be positive or negative.

covenants for title
The agreements entered into by the vendor giving the purchaser the right of action if the title proves bad under the Law of Property Act 1925, as amended.

cover flashing
See flashing

cowl
A cover fixed to the top of a chimney pot to prevent downdraughts and rainwater entering the flue.

craft
See trade.

crazing
Fine cracks that appear in a painted or plaster surface due to shrinkage on drying out.

creosote
A timber preservative obtained

from cold tar and generally used to treat rough timber used for sheds and fences. *See also* preservative.

cross wall construction
A series of main load-bearing walls comprising two end external walls and a number of internal walls built parallel to one another. The remaining external walls joining them are of a light non-load-bearing structure.

curing
A specified period of time required for concrete to set and harden to achieve its correct strength.

current
The flow of electrical energy in a circuit. *See also* circuit.

curtilage
The whole area of land and buildings within the boundaries of a property.

cut string
One that is cut to the profile of the treads and risers of a stair to support them. *See also* string.

cylinder
A copper tank which stores water fed from a cistern which is heated from a boiler or immersion heater.

cylinder latch
See cylinder lock.

cylinder lock
A door lock mechanism which is operated by a key which, when turned, releases or retracts a brass keeper allowing the door to be opened or locked. *See also* lock, latch, deadlock, mortice lock, night lock.

D

dado
A moulded timber rail fixed part way up an internal wall and separating the decorative finishes to the wall.

damages
The sum recoverable in a court action by one who has suffered a loss or injury. Damages are either liquidated or unliquidated. Liquidated damages are predetermined in an agreement and unliquidated are subject to the court's discretion.

damper
A device, incorporated in a flue, which can be adjusted to control the flow of air.

damping formula
A procedure used by the Department of the Environment to slow the effects of the Change to Housing Needs Indicator scores.

dampness
A condition caused by moisture, such as condensation, rising damp or rainwater penetration, through a wall or roof. Controlled by damp-proof courses, damp-proof membranes and vapour barriers.

damp-proof course
A waterproof barrier provided in a wall to prevent rising damp from the ground penetrating the walling above, which may result in internal damp. It is incorporated in external walls extending the full width of the wall or placed on both leaves of cavity walls and positioned a minimum of 150mm above ground level. It is also included in internal load-bearing walls and above window and door openings.

The material used must be impervious to the passage of water and would include engineering bricks, bituminous felt, PVC and metals.

The damp-proof course must be joined to a damp-proof membrane to provide a complete waterproof barrier to the whole area of the building. *See also* cavity tray, damp-proof membrane.

damp-proof membrane

A waterproof barrier that extends over the whole area of the building at ground level, with the purpose of preventing rising damp from the ground penetrating into the ground floor resulting in internal dampness.

It would normally be placed on top of a hardcore layer beneath a solid concrete floor slab and joined to the damp-proof course provided in the external and internal walls so that the whole area of the building is protected against rising damp. The material must be impervious to the passage of water, e.g. a heavy duty PVC sheet. Damp-proof membranes may be applied to existing concrete floors by spraying a liquid waterproof substance on to the surface or spreading asphalt over it. *See also* damp-proof course, tanking.

dancing step

One where the tread is narrower at one side but is fixed into a string.

dangerous premises

Under the Occupiers Liability Act 1957, as amended, the occupier owes a duty of care to lawful visitors. Compensation for loss to the visitor may be payable by the occupier and not the owner. This doctrine extends to trespassers.

dangerous structure notice

A notice, issued by the local authority, to a building owner requiring him to put a building into a safe condition.

date of valuation

A specific date stated on a valuation certificate which indicates the value of the building on that particular date.

datum

A line, point or level used to determine the positions of various parts of a building during construction. Benchmarks may be used to determine a datum. *See also* setting out, level.

daylight factor

Used to calculate the amount of

glazed area required to provide the required degree of natural illumination for a room. *See also* natural light, Waldram diagram.

daywork contract
A small works building contract where payment is based on hours worked, cost of materials, plant, transport and a percentage for the contractor's overheads and profit.

dead bolt
See deadlock.

dead light
See fixed light.

dead load
The load imposed on a building due to the weight of materials, fixtures and fittings. *See also* live load, total load, imposed load, vertical load.

deadlock
A door lock mechanism which is operated by a key which, when turned, releases or retracts a brass keeper. It is used for securing the door only. *See also* latch, lock, mortice lock, cylinder lock.

dead shore
A temporary support to an exist-

ing wall to allow an opening to be formed. It consists of two vertical props (dead shores) supporting the ends of a short beam (needle) which projects through a hole formed in the wall. *See also* raking shore, flying shore.

Deathwatch beetle
An insect that lives and feeds on hardwoods such as oak, particularly in old, decaying buildings.

debt
Money due from one person to another.

decibel
A unit of measurement of sound expressed in dB.

deciduous trees
Trees that shed their leaves each year and produce hardwoods such as oak and maple.

decking
Sheet material laid on top of joists to form floors and flat roofs.

deed
A document which must make clear that it is intended to be a deed and is validly executed as

such. For the deed to be executed it must be signed by an individual in the presence of witnesses who attest the signature and must be delivered by him or a person authorised by him or her.

deed of postponement
arrangement where the lending authority postpones its right to first claim on a housing association's funds in favour of another lender.

deemed planning permission
The situation under the Town and Country Planning Acts where planning permission is considered to have been granted without the necessity of formal approval from the local planning authority. *See also* General Development Order, permitted development.

deep seal trap
See water trap.

deep strip foundation
A narrow plain concrete continuous foundation in which the whole foundation trench is filled with concrete. It may prove more economical than widening a trench to allow working space to construct a nominal 150mm thick concrete strip. *See also* strip foundation.

defeasance
Termination of an estate.

default
The failure to do something required by the law, e.g. one party failing to meet the requirements of a specific court order.

defects liability period
The period agreed following the practical completion of building engineering, or other construction works, during which the contractor is obliged to make good any failure of materials or workmanship to meet the specific terms of the contract.

deferred interest mortgage
A mortgage when interest payment is delayed until well into the mortgage repayment period.

deflection
Movement caused by load, such as the bending of a beam.

deforcement
Wrongful holding of lands of another.

dehumidifier
A device that controls the amount of moisture in the air of one room by taking out water vapour thereby reducing humidity. *See also* air conditioning, humidity.

de ingressu
A writ of entry to property.

demise
The granting of a lease or the term of years granted.

demolition
The pulling down of a building or structure.

demolition order
An order of a local housing authority requiring the pulling down of a dwelling house which is unfit for human habitation, and which cannot be repaired at reasonable expense.

density
1. A term often used in town planning, meaning the number of dwelling units per area of land, often expressed as dwellings per acre or hectare.
2. The mass per unit volume of a material expressed in kg/m^3. *See also* bulk density.

Department of Social Security
The central government department responsible, *inter alia*, for income support and housing benefit.

Department of the Environment
Central government department responsible for housing.

deposit
1. The sum of money held on account to earn interest.
2. The placement of deeds of a mortgage property with the mortgagee.

deposit of title deeds
Delivery of same to creditor as security for debt, often a mortgage.

derelict
Buildings which have been abandoned or neglected.

descent
The passage of an interest in land, upon the death intestate of the owner, to a person or persons by virtue of consanguinity with the deceased.

design and build contract
A form of contractual agreement

for the undertaking of building, engineering or constructio works, which incorporates both the design and production phases of the operation.

design information

The information prepared by the design team, which is used by a contractor to carry out proposed building works. *See also* bill of quantities, drawings, specification.

design guide

A document, often associated with town planning, which offers guidance as to the type of buildings, or alterations to buildings, which would be acceptable within a defined area.

design mix

A specified mix for concrete to achieve the required strength and other qualities required.

design team

The people responsible for designing a building and producing the design information (drawings, specifications, bill of quantities) and is coordinated by the architect, including such persons as quantity surveyors and engineers. *See also* architect, quantity surveyor, engineer.

detached house

A dwelling that is complete in itself and is not joined to others. *See also* semi-detached house, terraced house.

detailed drawing

See drawings.

developer

A person or organisation who develops land or property for profit.

developer's profit

The portion of the value of a property accruing after allowing for the acquisition, construction costs, and other outlays of a developer.

developer's risk and profit

Often associated with the residual value method of property valuation, being the amount which is allowed to cover: first, an estimate of the sum needed to reflect the risk element between the valuation date and the completion of the development programme; and, second, an amount to meet the developer's requirements for profit on the venture.

development agent
In terms of the housing association movement, a housing association or a secondary co-operative which provides development services for smaller associations.

development brief
A document which contains a statement by the owner of a site suggesting detailed requirements for the proposed development to would-be developers.

development corporation
A corporate body, usually a public authority, charged with the development of a specific site, e.g. New Town Development Corporation.

development expenditure
The total sums of money expended by a developer in undertaking a development project. Normally divided into the cost of land acquired and the costs of construction.

development, permitted
Planning permission granted by a development order which does not require formal planning approval from a local planning authority. The Town and Country Planning General Permitted Development Order 1995 specifies certain classes of development which may be undertaken without formal permission. The relevant parts are as follows:

● development within the curtilage of a dwelling house
● minor operations
● changes of use
● temporary buildings and uses
● caravan sites
● agricultural buildings and operations
● forestry buildings and operations
● repairs to unadopted streets and private ways
● repairs to services
● demolition of buildings.

The Secretary of State has powers to remove certain of the above specified classes under what is termed an Article IV Direction.

development plan
A plan, usually associated with town planning, which indicates how the local planning authority would like to see a specific area developed in the future.

dew point
The temperature at which moist air condenses. *See also* condensation.

differential movement
See moisture movement, temperature movement, settlement.

differential settlement
Uneven settlement of a foundation. *See also* settlement.

dilapidations
The items of disrepair arising through breach of a contract, especially by one of the parties to a lease giving rise to a claim for remedial action or damages.

dilapidations report
A list or schedule of remedial work required to be carried out to an existing building, together with the costs involved. Normally compiled from a building survey.

dimension
The distance between two points and included on scale drawings to indicate lengths, widths and heights of various parts of the building.

direct access accommodation
Accommodation provided by way of a hostel for single people who are rootless.

direct cold water supply
A system for supplying cold water directly to the appliance from pipes connected to the rising main rather than from the cistern.

direct comparison method
A valuation method whereby the rental, or capital value of a property, is assessed, with regard to the prices or rents recently achieved by similar properties in a similar locality.

direct cylinder
A container for storing hot water that has been heated by a boiler rather than a heat exchanger. *See also* indirect cylinder, heat exchanger.

direct heating
The generation of heat into a room from an appliance such as a solid fuel, gas or electric fire, rather than from a central heating system.

direct hot water system
A system for supplying hot

water directly to an appliance that has been heated by a boiler rather than being supplied from a cylinder. *See also* combination boiler.

disclaimer
The renunciation of a claim or right.

discontinuance order
An order made by a local planning authority under the Town and Country Planning Act 1990, as amended, requiring the discontinuance of the lawful use of land or buildings. Compensation may be payable.

discount bonds
Bonds issued at below their redemption value. Used by the housing association movement.

discounting
A statistical procedure by which amounts of money, due to be received in the future, are brought to their current value on a specific valuation date allowing for accumulated interest at a selected rate which is assumed would be earned during the intervening period.

displacement pile
A pre-cast concrete pile in one

length or in sections driven into the ground by imparting blows on the pile head from a piling rig, or by using hydraulic methods. *See also* bearing pile.

distribution pipe
A pipe which supplies water to an appliance from a cistern.

district council
Outside metropolitan areas they are the local housing authority and often have their own stock of council housing.

district valuer
A public officer responsible for undertaking valuations for taxation, compulsory purchase and other statutory purposes on behalf of government departments or local authorities.

disturbance
Displacement of a person's home following compulsory purchase or possession secured by the landlord. Compensation may be payable to the displaced person.

disturbance payment
The amount of compensation payable by a local authority in pursuance of its statutory

powers. Often associated with compulsory purchase.

division wall
A wall used to separate rooms, such as a partition wall or one which separates buildings such as a party wall. *See also* internal wall, partition wall.

divorce value
Additional value released by the subdivision of property into two or more parts.

dog leg stair
Two flights of stairs between floors which are separated by a landing and are fixed in opposite directions so that a 180° turn is required to ascend or descend the particular flight. *See also* half landing.

domicile
Often associated with taxation purposes and being the country which is regarded as an individual's permanent home.

door
That which allows access to and from a building and to and from rooms. *See also* internal door, external door, fire door.

door casing
See door lining.

door closer
A spring device which automatically causes a door to close and is generally a requirement for fire doors.

doorframe
A timber surround to a door opening to which the door is fixed and normally used for external doors. It consists of either a solid rectangular section of timber or a hollow section of metal or plastic which is rebated to accommodate the door. It comprises two sides, a head and a sill.

door furniture
The mechanisms and accessories required for locking, opening and closing doors.

door head
The top member of a door frame.

door jamb
See door post.

door lining
A thin timber surround to a door opening to which the door is

fixed. It is normally used for internal doors, is equal to the wall and plaster thickness and lines the sides and top of the opening. *See also* doorframe.

door post
The side or vertical member of a door frame.

door sill
The bottom member of a door frame. *See also* sill.

door stop
The rebate in a door frame or lining, or timber strip planted into a lining to form a rebate that is used to accommodate the door and to provide a seal.

dormer
A window incorporated in a pitched roof and which projects beyond the roof slope so that it comprises two sides (cheeks) with a small flat roof. It is used where the roof space is to be used as a room.

dormer cheek
The side of a dormer.

dormer window
See dormer.

double door
Two doors each fixed to a common doorframe on one side and meeting in the centre.

double eaves course
Two courses of slates or tiles laid at the bottom edge or eaves of a roof. *See also* eaves course, under eaves course.

double floor
An upper timber joisted floor where an intermediate support (i.e. a beam) has been incorporated to support the joists at mid-span. *See also* single floor.

double glazing
Glass panels comprising two sheets of glass with a sealed air space between, which may be incorporated in doors and windows to reduce the transmission of heat and sound. *See also* sealed unit, secondary glazing.

double lap
See lap.

double roof
A roof comprising rafters to each roof slope with their ends fixed at the top (apex) and the bottom end supported on a wall (eaves) with a purlin support at

mid-span. *See also* purlin, pitched roof, trussed rafter, roof truss.

dovetail
A method of joining together two sections of wood by forming fan-shaped projections in one section and matching slots in the other.

dovetail joint
See dovetail.

dowel
A rounded timber or metal pin, one end of which is located into a predrilled hole in a component and the projection located into a similar predrilled hole of another component so that both components are joined.

downpipe
See surface water pipe.

drain
A pipe situated below ground level which is used for disposing foul and surface water from a building(s) within the boundary of a property and maintained by the owner(s).

drainage system
A series of pipes situated above

and below ground level and arranged to dispose foul and surface water from a building(s) within the boundary of a property and maintained by the owner(s).

drainpipe
See drain.

drain plug
A device used for blocking the end of a drainage run to allow for testing.

drain tests
The procedures involved in determining whether drains are watertight and free from blockage. *See also* hydraulic test, air test, smoke test.

draw down
The release of finance, often at various stages, for development projects, provided by way of a loan, often for large sums, over a long period of time.

drawing board
A plastic or wooden board used for producing drawings. *See also* T-square, set square.

drawings
Part of the design information

which are dimensional details of the proposed building drawn to scale and including elevations, sections and plans. *See also* orthographic projection, isometric projection, perspective drawing.

drip
See check throat.

driven pile
See displacement pile.

dry construction
A method of using factory-produced components, such as prefabricated partitions, which are assembled and fixed in position on-site as opposed to constructing in situ using bricks, mortar and plaster which require water for mixing. *See also* wet construction, in situ.

drying shrinkage
The process that occurs in materials, such as plaster, which contain water used for mixing that causes shrinkage on drying, leaving fine cracks at the surface.

dry lining
A dry construction method of providing an internal finish to a wall, which consists of fixing plasterboard sheets into a framework attached to the wall. An insulation layer may be incorporated and foil-backed plasterboard used to act as a vapour barrier. *See also* gypsum wallboard, foil-backed plasterboard, vapour barrier.

dry rot
A condition which causes timber to decay due to damp conditions, such as inadequately ventilated suspended timber ground floors. It is a fungus (*merulius lacrymans* or *serpula lacrymans*) which has a pungent odour. *See also* wet rot.

duality of interest
When an individual who may be serving as an officer or member of a housing association receives payment or benefit from the association beyond his normal contract of employment with the association.

duct
Provision for carrying services, such as pipes and cables, to a building and within a building.

dumpy level
A level which has a fixed verti-

cal axis but requires adjustment to the horizontal axis. *See also* level.

durability

The capability of a material to withstand deterioration from outside sources, such as frost. *See also* frost action.

dwarf wall

See sleeper wall.

dwelling

1. A building used for residential purposes.
2. Defined under the Rent Act 1977 as 'a house, or part of a house'. Defined under the Housing Act 1985 as 'premises used, or suitable for use, as a separate dwelling'. Under the Landlord and Tenant Act 1985 defined as 'a building or part of a building occupied, or intended to be occupied as a separate dwelling, together with any yard, garden, outhouses and the pertinencies belonging to it, or usually enjoyed with it'.

dwelling house

Defined under the Housing Act 1985, in reference to secure tenancies, as 'a house or part of a house'.

E

earth
A term used to describe soil.

earthenware
Clay products that are burnt to lower temperatures than stoneware. *See also* stoneware.

easement
A right by an owner of land over land owned by someone else. The right may include water, light, etc. The land owned by the possessor of the easement is called the dominant tenement, and the servient tenement is the land owner over which the right is enjoyed.

A positive easement consists of a right to do something on the land of another and a negative easement restricts the use the owner of the servient tenement may make of his land. *See also* quasi-easement.

easement of light
See easement *and* light.

eaves
The bottom portion of a roof which normally projects over the face of the wall. It may be boxed in (closed eaves) with a fascia board and soffit board fixed to brackets, or the rafters of the roof may be left exposed (open eaves). *See also* closed eaves, open eaves, sprocketed eaves, overhanging eaves.

eaves course
Roof slates and tiles placed at the bottom part of the roof so that they project over the eaves gutter for surface water disposal purposes. *See also* double eaves course, under eaves course.

eaves fascia
See fascia board.

eaves gutter

A half-rounded pipe fixed to the eaves of a roof, the purpose of which is to collect surface water from the roof and convey it to a surface water pipe to which it is connected. *See also* gutter, box gutter.

eaves height

Internally, the difference in level between the floor surface and the underside of the roof covering, supporting purlins or underlining at the eaves on the internal wall face. Externally, the difference in level between the ground surface and the exterior of the roof covering at the eaves on the external wall face, ignoring any parapet.

eaves plate

See wall plate.

eaves tile

A short-length tile used as part of the eaves course to maintain the required lap.

eccentric load

A vertical load that is not centrally supported on a foundation.

economic life

The time during which the value of buildings or a site, in any particular use, is greater than the value of the site for any other feasible purposes, including redevelopment.

edging strip

A thin strip of timber fixed to the edges of a door to cover the core. *See also* door.

effective span

The distance between the centre of supports. *See also* span, clear span.

efflorescence

Salt crystals which appear on the external surface of brickwork and concrete in the form of a white powder. It is caused by sulphates in the material which dissolve in absorbed rainwater and crystallise at the surface upon drying.

elderly persons' dwellings

Residential units suitable for active elderly people, designed in accordance with the Housing Corporation's Design Guidelines on Sheltered Housing and Mobility Standards. *See also* mobility housing, frail elderly housing, special needs housing.

electric current

See current.

electric immersion heater
See immersion heater.

electricity distribution
The use of the electricity supply to provide electricity to individual properties via substations.

electricity supply
The national system used to provide electrical power to the whole country.

electro-osmosis
A system used to control the passage of water through porous materials, e.g. rising damp. It is a method used for providing a damp-proof course to an existing building and consists of a copper strip through which an electrical current is passed which causes water to flow away from the wall.

element
A component part of a building such as a wall, floor or roof.

elevation
A drawing which represents to scale the completed building as viewed from the front, rear and sides. *See also* drawing.

emery cloth
See glass paper.

emissivity
The amount of heat radiated by a surface.

emphyteusis
The grant of land for ever for an annual rent paid to the grantor and his successors.

emulsion paint
A substance applied to internal plaster wall surfaces for decorative purposes and consisting of synthetic polymers dispersed in water so that the drying process is by means of water evaporation, leaving a slightly porous surface. *See also* paint.

enabling Act or statute
An Act of Parliament which allows a local, or public authority or government department to use its powers of compulsory purchase to acquire land for particular specified purposes.

enactment
See Act of Parliament.

encroachment
The unauthorised extension of the boundaries of a piece of land over adjoining land which is in the ownership of another person.

encumbrance
Charge or liability attached to land such as a mortgage.

endowment
Funds, or property, which are placed in trust for a specific purpose.

endowment trust
A portfolio or fund established and held in trust for the maintenance, repair and upkeep of (usually) inherited property.

energy management
The systematic and rational approach to the provision and conservation of the use of energy in a building. Often associated with careful measurement and monitoring to ensure that any changes increase energy efficiency.

enforcement notice
A notice served by the local planning authority under the Town and Country Planning Act 1990 as amended, requiring that development which is unauthorised must cease or be removed. If it is not, then it becomes a criminal offence. *See also* Planning and Compensation Act 1991.

enfranchisement
The acquisition of the freehold or extension of the lease by a tenant holding a lease exceeding 21 years at a rent of less than two-thirds of the rateable value.

engineer
A qualified person who would be responsible for producing part of the design information, such as structural details (i.e. a structural engineer), electrical details (i.e. an electrical engineer) and heating and services details (i.e. a heating engineer). *See also* design team.

engineering bricks
Manufactured from clays rich in iron oxides and are burnt to high temperatures to produce a dense, strong brick with a vitrified interior. Used where heavy loads have to be supported and for work below ground level where water pressures have to be resisted. *See also* brick, clay bricks, common bricks, facing bricks.

English bond
The arrangement of bricks to produce alternate courses of headers and stretchers within a wall. *See also* header, stretcher,

English garden wall bond, Flemish bond, garden wall bond.

English garden wall bond
A form of English bond but where the arrangement of bricks is such that the course of headers is positioned at every fourth to sixth course of stretchers. *See also* English bond, header, stretcher.

entail
A right in land only inheritable by lineal descendant.

entry
Going on to land with a clear intention of asserting a right on it.

envelope
1. The parts of a building or structure which enclose it – e.g. roof, walls, windows, doors – which, together, form its external envelope.
2. In planning terms, often refers to the boundary around a particular piece of land.

environmental envelope
The enclosing element of a building separating natural and artificial environments. As such, it must satisfy certain criteria in terms of appearance, strength, stability, durability and fire, thermal and sound resistance. *See also* external wall.

epitome of title
A listing of documents to establish the root of a title to land.

equilibrium
The state at which, when a building component is subject to load, it does not move.

equitable
Associated with the rules of the law of equity.

equitable easement
An easement other than one created by a deed, prescription or statute, e.g. an easement lasting for life.

equitable estate
An exclusive equitable right to land, but referred to since 1925 as an equitable interest.

equitable interest
A charge, or interest on land, other than a legal estate.

equity
1. The part of the law which

recognises concepts and doctrines and grants remedies not acknowledged by the common law.

2. A colloquial term describing the inherent value of a property which is realised, after paying off the liabilities, when it is sold.

equity finance

Sums of money advanced in the form of a loan normally made available to a company for a specific venture, such as the development of land. The contract normally entitles the person to a share of any profit.

equity-linked mortgage

A mortgage whereby the interest on the principal, in part or in whole, is calculated usually yearly by reference to changes in the annual return on the security.

erosion

The wearing away of the surface of a material over a period of time as a result of exposure to extremes of weather.

escape route

See means of escape.

escape stairs

See fire escape stairs.

escrow

A deed which is sealed, signed and conditionally delivered, but will not become operative until a condition has been met.

escutcheon

A metal keyhole plate fixed to a door.

estate

1. The right to use land for a certain period of time.

2. A section of land normally in one ownership, e.g. landed estates, a university estate, etc.

estate action

A programme administered by the Department of the Environment to fund the refurbishment and rebuilding of dilapidated inner city housing estates owned by local authorities and housing associations.

estate agency work

Under section 1 of the Estate Agent's Act 1979 defined as 'things done by a person in the course of business pursuant to instructions received from a client who wishes to dispose of, or acquire an interest in land'.

estate agent

A person who advises the principal in respect of the sale, purchase, lettings, mortgages, etc. *See also* estate agency work.

estate, legal
Under section 1 of the Law of Property Act 1925 the only legal estates capable of subsisting are an estate in fee simple (freehold) and a term of years absolute (leasehold).

estate owner
The owner of a legal estate in land.

estate tail
An estate enduring so long as the original owner has a lineal descendant on his death.

estate terrier
An estate management information system used for the efficient day-to-day running of an estate. Usually includes details of estate boundaries, details of titles, lettings, easements, etc.

evasion
A colloquial term often used to mean an illegal act or omission resulting from the production of false information in relation to taxation.

evergreen
A type of short-term loan offered by merchant banks in which a fixed sum is borrowed for a rolling period, with an annual option to sustain it for a further period and with variable interest rates.

eviction
Recovery or repossession of land and property with or without the due process of law. The Protection from Eviction Act 1977, as amended, makes the eviction of a residential occupier a criminal offence unless resulting from court proceedings.

excavation
The process involved in removing earth for such purposes as building foundations.

excavator
A machine used for excavating earth.

excess charge
A sum levied by the landlord at the end of the year for the amounts due and recoverable legally from the tenant under the terms of the lease applied in relation to the provision of services provided for the tenant during the said period.

exchange of contracts
The initial formal and legally enforceable step in the transfer of land or property.

exclusive rent
The rent, under a lease, which makes the tenant solely responsible for the payment of rates, services and other outgoings.

executor
Person named in a will whom the testator wishes to administer the estate.

exemption
The mechanism which removes legal obligations or financial liability imposed by common law, or statute.

exempt lease
A lease exempted from the security of tenure provisions of the Landlord and Tenant Act 1954, following a joint application to the court by the landlord and the tenants.

ex gratia
Something carried out without legal obligation or the admission of liability.

ex gratia payment
A sum of money paid usually by a public authority, where there is no strict entitlement to compensation.

existing use rights
A colloquial term used to describe the uses of land and buildings which do not require planning permission. The uses are those contained in the Use Classes Order, the General Development Order or have existing use certificates attaching to them. *See also* existing use value, Use Classes Order, General Development Order.

existing use value
1. A colloquial term meaning the open market value of land or buildings applied to their current use as opposed to any potential use.
2. The value which may apply to a situation where compensation is payable because the Secretary of State declines to confirm a purchase notice and instead directs that planning permission should be granted for some other form of development as per the Town and Country Planning Act 1990, as amended by the Planning and Compensation Act 1991.

expanded metal lathing
A steel mesh which is fixed to a timber framework, or similar, and used to support plaster.

expansion joint
Provision made between two constructions, such as walls and floors, to allow movement to take place. *See also* moisture movement, temperature movement, settlement.

ex parte
On behalf of one side only.

expert
A person having particular specialised knowledge. *See also* independent expert.

expropriation
The compulsory acquisition of an estate or part of an estate by the nation.

external audit
An independent examination of the financial accounts of an organisation.

external door
One that allows access to and from a building and must be more durable than an internal door. It may be flush with a solid core comprising vertical timber strips glued together and faced both sides with plywood and may incorporate a glazed panel, or be panelled comprising a solid timber frame incorporating glazed and solid timber panels. External doors are also manufactured from aluminium and plastic. *See also* internal door, fire door.

external enclosure
See external wall.

external value
Under the Royal Institution of Chartered Surveyors *Guidance Notes on the Valuation of Assets*, defined as a qualified valuer who is not an internal valuer and where neither he nor any of his partners or co-directors are directors or employees of the company, or of another company within a group of companies, or having a significant financial interest in the company or group, or where neither the company nor the group has a significant financial interest in the valuer's firm or company. The company may include a housing association, development company, etc.

external wall
The external enclosure to a building constructed of masonry. It supports upper floors and the roof and incorporates windows and doors. *See also* environmental envelope, wall.

extinguishment
The termination of a right or obligation.

F

fabric heat loss
Heat energy that is lost through the fabric of the building from the inside to the outside through the walls, floors and roof. It is dependent upon the difference between the outside and inside temperatures, the 'U' value and area of the building element. *See also* thermal heat transmission coefficient, heat loss, infiltration heat loss.

façade
The front elevation or external face of a building.

facing bricks
Clay bricks which are sand faced and textured on one length face and both end faces to give a variety of colours and textures. Stronger and more durable than common bricks but more expensive. Used for external walls where appear-ance is important, and may also be used for internal walls to be left exposed. *See also* brick, clay bricks, common bricks, engineering bricks.

faience
A clay block with a glazed finish used as a facing to external walls. *See also* terracotta.

factor of safety
A figure that may be used to increase variable load for design purposes.

fair faced
An internal brick or block wall left exposed and where the joints are neatly pointed.

fair rent
The fixing by a rent officer, under various Rent Acts, of a 'fair rent' for certain types of residential tenancy.

fall

The slope or gradient provided to a flat roof for surface water drainage purposes.

false ceiling

See suspended ceiling.

fanlight

A window incorporated in a door frame and positioned above an external door to allow the passage of natural light and also, in some cases, to provide natural ventilation. *See also* borrowed light.

fascia board

A timber board fixed to the bottom end of roof rafters to form part of an eaves construction. *See also* eaves.

fat lime

See high calcium line.

fee simple

A freehold interest in land.

fellow

The most senior member of a professional organisation, e.g. Fellow of the Royal Institution of Chartered Surveyors.

felt

See bitumastic felt.

fender wall

A wall surrounding a hearth to a fireplace and supporting the joists of a hollow ground floor.

fenestration

The window arrangement in the external walls of a building.

ferrous metal

A mixture of metals containing a high proportion of iron, e.g. steel.

feu

Perpetual lease at a fixed rent.

fibreboard

A composite sheet made from wood fibres glued and bonded together to produce a variety of standard sheets, such as hardboards and insulation boards. *See also* hardboard, insulation board.

fibreglass

See glass wool.

fidelity guarantee

An insurance against financial loss resulting from fraud or dishonesty committed by officers or employees of housing associations.

fiduciary

The relationship whereby one person is required to exercise the rights and powers for the benefit of another.

field drain

See land drain.

fillet

A substance used for covering joints, e.g. a cement fillet used to cover the joint between the edge of an external path at its junction with an external wall.

final account

The agreed statement of the amount of money to be paid at the end of a building contract.

final certificate

A certificate indicating the completion of a building contract, normally issued by an architect or surveyor.

final coat

The top coat of a plastered, rendered or painted surface.

Financial Provision Orders

Court orders attached to the granting of decrees of divorce, nullity or separation and concerning payments by one spouse to another or the children. Under the Matrimonial and Family Proceedings Act 1984 and the Child Support Act 1991, as amended, the court, in making the orders for periodic or lump sum payments, must give first consideration to the welfare of children under 18 and, if possible, seek to achieve a clean break.

financial viability returns

In a housing association context, the housing corporation requires all housing associations seeking a development allocation to produce financial viability returns. They are intended to demonstrate the extent to which associations have the resources to cover the financial risks involved in undertaking various types of development and taking out long-term loans.

financial year

1. The period of 12 calendar months from 1 April to 31 March.
2. For other purposes, often a period of 12 calendar months stated in the articles or memorandum of agreement of a company.

finder's fee

A sum payable to an agent employed to find a property on behalf of a client.

fine aggregate

Constituent part of a concrete mix which is used to contribute to the strength and to fill the voids (spaces) between the coarse aggregate to give density and consists of grit sand.

Also used for cement and plaster mortars where a finer sand would be used.

finial

An ornamental feature fixed at the apex of a gable roof in the shape of a moulded point or ball.

finish coat

See final coat.

finishes

The internal coverings of a building, not forming part of its structure.

fink truss

See trussed rafter.

firebrick

A clay unit, fixed in a fireplace, and providing the area for burn-

ing. It is connected to the flue and shaped to produce effective combustion.

fire check door

See fire door.

fire door

A solid core flush door which may incorporate a reinforced glass panel which is capable of resisting fire for a certain period of time, (e.g. ½ hr, 1 hr). *See also* core.

fire escape stairs

A stairway to provide an escape route between floors and landings in case of fire and situated within or on the outside of a building. *See also* stairs.

fire insurance

Insurance taken out to cover loss or damage to property resulting from fire.

fire officer

An officer of the local authority whose duties are to inspect buildings and evaluate means of escape and fire precaution methods.

fireplace

A recessed opening in the internal face of an external wall to provide a means for burning solid fuel for heating purposes.

fire protection
The required provision of a building, within its design and construction, to adequately prevent fire spreading within and without for a certain period of time and to allow the building to be safely vacated in the event of fire, and to provide for means of escape, smoke detection and fire-fighting apparatus.

fire resistance
The capability of a material or element to resist fire for a specified period of time before collapsing. *See also* non-combustible, non-flammable.

fire stop
A barrier, such as a suspended ceiling, provided in a void to prevent fire spread.

fire surround
A decorative feature, normally formed from masonry or glazed tiles, to a fireplace.

firrings
Tapered strips of timber placed on top of roof joists to give the

required gradient or fall to a flat roof.

first angle projection
See orthographic projection.

first floor
The floor immediately above the ground floor. *See also* upper floor.

fit for habitation
Implied statutory covenant attached to certain low rent tenancies.

fitting
An item used for joining components, e.g. a compression fitting for joining pipes.

fixed charge
A charge paid by the lender as security for a loan.

fixed light
Part of a window that does not open. *See also* opening light, casement window.

fixed load
See dead load.

fixed price contract
Where the total price is fixed at the beginning of a building con-

tract, subject to variations or fluctuations in stated circumstances. *See also* contract, prime cost contract, cost plus contract.

fixed rent
A rent which cannot be moved upwards or downwards during the stated time period in a lease.

fixed term
A lease or tenancy for a set period. The date of commencement and termination must be agreed before there can be a legally binding agreement.

fixture
The permanent part of a building usually associated with internal items such as the bathroom and kitchen fittings.

fixtures
Those elements of a building which are commonly regarded as easily removed.

flame spread
See spread of flame.

flammability
The ease with which a material will burn.

flashing
A waterproof covering dressed over an upstand formed against a wall, such as that provided to a flat roof. *See also* stepped flashing, upstand.

flat
The subdivision of premises in residential occupation usually on the same floor and forming part of the same building, divided horizontally from some other part of it.

flat arch
See arch.

flat gauged arch
See arch.

flat roof
One that is inclined at an angle of less than 10° and is covered with a waterproof layer such as bitumastic felt rather than slates and tiles. *See also* pitched roof, bitumastic felt, welted drip.

Flemish bond
The arrangement of bricks so that each course comprises a header followed by a stretcher within a wall. *See also* header, stretcher, English bond, English garden wall bond, garden wall bond.

Flemish garden wall bond
See garden wall bond.

flexible mortgage
A mortgage in which the initial repayments are negotiable, usually maintained at a low level and can be switched to a fixed interest mortgage within specified times during the longer term.

flight
A series of steps between floors and landings.

flitch beam
Two timber joists bolted together to form a beam used to support an upper internal wall or as an intermediate support in double floor construction.

float coat
The second or undercoat of plaster. *See also* render coat.

float glass
Manufactured by pouring molten glass on to a bed of molten metal so that it floats on the surface and then polishing the upper surface by flame. It is then passed over rollers into a cooling chamber. *See also* glass.

floating charge
A charge which a lender, for security for a loan, can spread over the borrower's assets.

floor
A level surface situated within a building whose function is to provide structural stability, prevent the passage of dampness, provide thermal, sound and fire resistance, and give a durable pleasing appearance. *See also* ground floor, upper floor, open floor, sprung floor, solid ground floor, hollow ground floor, strip floor.

floor area
The total superficial area of a building including all floors. The Royal Institution of Chartered Surveyors Code of Measuring Practice distinguishes the following categories: first, gross external area; second, gross internal area; third, net internal area.

floorboards
A covering to timber joisted floors comprising strips of timber approximately 150mm wide and 20mm thick with tongued and grooved edges which are cramped together and nailed to

flushing cistern

A water tank positioned above a WC that is operated by a lever or chain that allows an amount of water to be discharged into the WC pan to clear the waste. *See also* automatic flushing cistern, low level flushing cistern, water closet.

flush pointing

See mortar joint.

flying shore

A temporary support system to an existing wall that requires strengthening, which is attached to the walls of opposite buildings above ground level while maintaining access below. It consists of a main horizontal member (flying shore) with inclined members attached to the wall at one end and the horizontal member at the other, fixed each side above and below. *See also* dead shore, raking shore, shore.

foil-backed plasterboard

Plasterboard sheets with aluminium foil bonded on one side to act as a vapour barrier. *See also* aluminium foil.

footing

The widening of a solid brick wall at the base to spread the load on the foundation upon which it is supported by creating a series of steps.

force

The effect of load that causes the fibres of a material to be in a state of compression or tension. *See also* compression, tension.

forced sale value

The Royal Institution of Chartered Surveyors *Guidance Notes on the Valuation of Assets* define it as 'open market value, but with the proviso that the vendor has imposed a time limit for completion, which cannot be regarded as a reasonable period in which to negotiate the sale, taking into account the nature of the property and the state of the market'.

foreclosure

The situation under the Law of Property Act 1925 where a mortgagee has restricted power to extinguish the mortgagor's right of redemption by transfer of the mortgagor's interest in the property to himself, provided the mortgagor defaults in payment of dues, or in complying with any other terms of the mortgage deed.

foreshore
Part of the seashore lying between mean high and mean low tide lines. It is normally held that the foreshore is owned by the Crown.

forfeiture
The process whereby a landlord exercises his right to retake physical possession of premises and thus extinguish a lease following the tenant's failure to remedy a breach of the terms of that lease.

formal tender
A formal bid made by a tenderer. *See also* tender, tendering process.

formation level
The level produced after stripping off the vegetable layer from the ground to expose the subsoil which is the layer upon which the building is constructed. *See also* subsoil, vegetable layer.

Formica
A laminated plastic sheet used for facing surfaces such as kitchen fittings.

formwork
Temporary support for in situ reinforced concrete work such as foundations, and which is removed when the concrete has hardened.

forward finance
The forward commitment where an amount of money is made available and is repaid relatively quickly thereafter from the proceeds of a sale.

forward letting/sale
An arrangement where agreement is entered into for the taking of a lease or purchase of property in advance of completion of the development.

foul drain
A pipe situated below ground level which is used for disposing foul water from a building(s) within the boundary of a property and maintained by the owner(s).

foul sewer
A pipe situated below ground level used for disposing of foul water from foul drains and transferring it to a sewage treatment plant and which is the

responsibility of the water authority.

foul water
The waste water flow from soil and waste fittings such as WCs, baths and sinks.

foundation
That part of the building which supports the total load and transfers it to the subsoil. *See also* strip foundation, wide strip foundation, wild strip foundation, raft foundation, beam and pile foundation, ground beam.

frail elderly housing
In the housing association context, housing for frail elderly people. It includes housing which provides personal care and support for this category of person. *See also* elderly persons' dwellings, mobility housing.

frame
An arrangement of metal or timber which forms a basis for fixing a sheet covering to form a structure such as a partition.

framed door
See battened door, panelled door.

framed partition
See stud partition.

frank-fee
Freehold land.

frank tenement
Freehold.

fraudulent conveyance
A transfer of land without consideration and with intent to defraud a subsequent purchaser. Such actions are voidable by the purchaser under the Law of Property Act 1925.

freedom from encumbrance
Land and property free from any binding rights of parties other than the owner.

freehold
The most complete form of ownership of land. A legal estate in fee simple.

French casement
A combination of windows and doors as one unit normally comprising a pair of glazed doors with casement windows each side.

French drain
A trench filled with brick or similar rubble used to drain ground

water and direct it to a discharge point such as an open ditch. *See also* land drain.

French window

See French casement.

friction pile

An in situ concrete pile which supports and transfers the load from a building to the ground by virtue of its shape and frictional resistance, and is not supported on a load-bearing stratum. *See also* bored pile.

friendly societies

Organisations registered under the Friendly Societies Act 1977, as amended, to provide, by means of voluntary contributions, for the relief of members and their families during times of sickness, old age etc. They are unincorporated mutual insurance associations which possess mortgage lending powers.

frieze

That part of the wall below a cornice.

frontage

The length of a plot of land, or building, measured along the road to which the plot of land or building fronts.

frontager

Owner or occupier of land which abuts a highway, seashore or river.

front money

Sums of money made available usually as initial short-term finance for the development of land. Often the short-term finance involves the interest being rolled up during the construction period of the development project.

frost action

The effect of absorbed water expanding upon freezing and exerting pressure within a material, such as bricks and concrete, resulting in cracking and flaking at the surface. *See also* durability.

frost heave

The effect of ground water freezing and exerting pressure on external walls due to the expansion of the frozen water.

full management

A situation where all aspects of property management are the responsibility of a managing agent.